Experiments in the Physiology
of
Human Performance

Experiments in the Physiology of Human Performance

By BENJAMIN RICCI

Director, Laboratory of Applied Physiology
Boyden Gymnasium
University of Massachusetts
Amherst, Massachusetts

Lea & Febiger

Philadelphia, 1970

SBN 8121–0286–X

Library of Congress Catalog Card Number: 76–102701

Printed in the United States of America

PREFACE

"Without laboratories men of science are soldiers without arms."
Louis Pasteur (1822–1895)

Experiments in the Physiology of Human Performance has been prepared for students of many disciplines—medicine, industrial engineering, physical education, nursing, dietetics, physical therapy, and physiology. Its purpose is to acquaint its users with the mechanics of experimentation—ranging from literature search to calibration, from gas analysis to graphical portrayal.

For a number of reasons the preparation of this text presented challenges, principal among which was my awareness of the *diversity of purpose* and *scarcity of apparatus* which characterize many rooms designated as "human factors" laboratories, or as laboratories for the study of human physical and physiological performance.

Surveys of laboratory apparatus available to students for the assessment of human physiological performance have yielded uniform results in that they have revealed an abundance of stopwatches and stethoscopes, and a scarcity of gas analyzers and electronic monitoring apparatus. Adequate apparatus for the estimation of many parameters and variables of small mammals, fishes, amphibians, or reptiles characterizes departments of biology and zoology; however, only infrequently is such apparatus suited to the task of assessing human performance.

It must not be assumed that the laboratory apparatus essential to the emphasis in this text are prohibitively expensive. Available from many sources, for example, are oxygen-carbon dioxide analyzers, priced at approximately $200, which offer precision capability comparable to that of the most expensive apparatus. Obviously, when compared with more expensive types, the low priced analyzers possess certain disadvantages, such as decreased ease of operation, requirement of more time for gas analysis, lack of continuous read-out capability, or loss of capability for simultaneous computer analysis of data—in short, they are less convenient.

Throughout this text, one major emphasis has been presented—that of featuring intellectually stimulating and challenging laboratory exercises

v

22683

which can be conducted with a minimum of expense. The approximate cost of the apparatus suggested is $5,500. This figure can be trimmed. For example, one can weigh the reagents necessary for gas analysis apparatus on precision analytic balances located in or borrowed from the chemistry laboratory, thereby significantly reducing financial outlay.

Measurement is approximate, not exact; in the laboratory, error sources abound. Recognition of these sources is stressed in an effort to obtain data that will as far as possible be precise (minutely exact) as opposed to approximate (nearly exact).

For the most part, metric terminology has been used; however, English units are occasionally "mixed-in," especially in the Appendix. This is unavoidable, for one cannot order apparatus from an American laboratory supplier without resorting to predominately English units, with but an occasional smattering of metric units. Sometimes, the mixture ("metglish") is amusing. Note this catalogue description of a major American supplier for glass tubing:: "In lengths of 4 ft. Sizes 2mm and 3mm are packed in cases of 5 lbs. and 15 lbs."

The following persons have read and commented on the applicability and challenge of particular sections: Miss Marilyn Cairns, Department of Physical Education for Women, Boston-Bouvé College, Northeastern University; Mr. Richard V. Jackman, R.P.T. Chief, Physical Therapy, Franklin County Hospital, Greenfield, Massachusetts; Dr. Robert Kertzer, University of New Hampshire at Durham; Dr. Frank Pleasants, The University of North Carolina at Greensboro; Dr. Richard Trueswell, Head, Department of Industrial Engineering, University of Massachusetts; Dr. Benjamin Davies, University of Birmingham, England, Visiting Professor (Human Factors), University of Massachusetts at Amherst; and Professor Roger Williams, Eastern Michigan University at Ypsilanti. Their comments enabled me to gauge more effectively the local problems and differing disciplinary approaches. I am deeply appreciative of their efforts.

My expression of gratitude is extended to Miss Phyllis Joyce and Mr. Martin C. Hubbard, reference librarians of the University of Massachusetts Library, whose assistance was cheerfully and competently extended.

To Mr. Donald Curtis, a skillful illustrator, and to Mr. Russ Mariz, University Staff Photographer, special thanks are due.

The understanding and cooperation of Dr. Ruth Abernathy, Mr. John Febiger Spahr, Miss Emily Anderson, and Mr. Thomas Colaiezzi of Lea & Febiger are appreciated.

May this publication enrich the laboratory and research life of the user.

Amherst, Massachusetts   BENJAMIN RICCI

CONTENTS

1. *Introduction* 1

2. *Somatometry* 17

3. *Cardiac Performance and Response to Exercise* 35

4. *Analysis of Gross Muscle Function* 53

5. *Reaction Time (RT) and Movement Time (MT)* 73

6. *Assessing Joint Range of Movement* 89

7. *Regulatory Mechanism: Heat and Water Loss* 103

8. *Assessing Respiratory Volumes* 123

9. *Assessing Metabolic Function: Indirect Calorimetry* 143

   Appendix A 165

   Appendix B 195

   Index 205

LABORATORY EXERCISES

1. Estimation of Body Fat, Behnke Technique 20

2. Estimation of Body Surface Area: DuBois Height-Weight Formula 25

3. Estimation of Specific Gravity: Archimedian Principle, Behnke, Feen, and Welham Technique 27

4. Estimation of Systolic and Diastolic Blood Pressure and the Recording and Demonstration of Variability of Cardiac Frequency and Pulse Rate 39

5. The Hyman Index: An Index of the Adjustment Capability of the Heart 43

6. The Carlson Fatigue Curve Test 45

7. Cardiac Adjustment to Change in Rate and Amount of Work 47

8. Interrelationship of Load and Cadence to Girth of Forearm Flexors 57

9. Force Analysis in Knee Extension 65

10. Measuring Reaction Time (RT) and Movement Time (MT) 75

11. Effect of Heat and of Cold on Reaction Time and Movement Time of Preferred Limb 79

12. Effect of Normal versus Reduced Blood Flow in Upper Limb on Reaction Time and Movement Time 82

13. Estimation of Range of Movement of Left Knee and Ankle during Bench Stepping 91

14. Heat Production and Avenues of Heat Loss during Exercise .. 107

15. Sweat Loss and Composition 112

16. Effect of Exercise on Urine Volume and Composition 116

17. Subdivisions of Lung Volume Taken in the Erect Standing Position 127

18. Vital Capacity: One-Stage, Two-Stage, Timed, Predicted. Comparisons of Minute Volume Measurement 132

19. Effect of Various Gas Mixtures on External Respiration 139

20. Calculating Oxygen Consumption $\dot{V}O_2$, Ventilation Equivalent for Oxygen VEO_2, and Reciprocal of VEO_2, by means of Closed-Circuit Systems 146

21. Calculating Oxygen Consumption by the Open-Circuit Method 149

22. Step Test: A Physiological Appraisal 158

1

INTRODUCTION

"It is not so important to be serious as it is to be serious about the important things. The monkey wears an expression of seriousness which would do credit to any scholar, but the monkey is serious because it itches." ROBERT MAYNARD HUTCHINS[9]

Laboratory exercises can be enjoyable as well as meaningful. For maximum reenforcement of learning, thorough, *pre-lab preparation* is required of the student. Only through such an approach—an attitude—can the student focus on the physiological principles and concepts being demonstrated. Assignments must not only be read, they must be *mastered*. Because mathematical calculations play a major role in expressing results, the student is urged to review and master slide-rule operation.* In addition, the student is expected to review such uncomplicated mathematical manipulations as expressing results in percent, or of converting liters to milliliters, or centimeters to decimeters—all accomplished by moving the decimal point from one position to another. The language of the metric system is used throughout this book, hence, this system of measurement must be mastered.†

Preparation for each laboratory exercise involves careful reading of the assignment in *Physiological Basis of Human Performance* followed by thorough reading of each laboratory assignment in its entirety—from introductory paragraphs to *Concluding Remarks*. Use of index and appendix is suggested.

The ensuing discussion relates specifically to topics that are essential

---

* See text pages 243–245. NB: Throughout this publication, "text" refers to *Physiological Basis of Human Performance* by B. Ricci (Philadelphia, Lea & Febiger, 1967).

† See text pages 286–289.

to a full laboratory experience. No significance should be attached to the order of presentation.

In the hope that research interest is stimulated and with the realization that term papers or laboratory reports may be required, discussions of *Literature Search* and of *Graph Construction* are presented.

Obviously, each of the considerations presented is important; however, of fundamental importance is the topic *Calibration*. Indefensible is the structure of any laboratory session which leaves little room for the skeptic to operate or which permits blind faith in the absolute and repeat accuracy of the apparatus. In experimentation, calibration is not only fundamental but also of utmost import.

Literature Search

Documentation is an important part of a detailed laboratory report and is an essential part of a research paper. A term paper of merit reflects a review of relevant articles from a variety of scientific journals.

Because of the interdisciplinary nature of exercise physiology, familiarity with library procedures is essential. Pertinent information is international in scope. Selected articles, initially presented in foreign languages, are frequently available in translation. Use of foreign language dictionaries affords the student an opportunity of translating short captions from graphs which themselves are universal in character.

Literature search may begin with a perusal of journal indices or reference lists accompanying chapters in exercise physiology or physiology texts. Or, the search may begin with a check of the library card catalogs.

Catalog cards are filed in a manner convenient for the user, i.e., *books* may be located (1) by author and title or (2) by subject, the two catalogs being physically separated and usually distinctively labeled. On occasion, use can be made of such publications as *Books in Print*[4] and the author-title-series index.

Browsing in the stack area is not the most efficient means of locating books; however, the yield from such a technique is increased if the user can confine his browsing to the more promising areas. For the users of this publication, such stack areas are designated by the Q or R classes of the Library of Congress: Q = major classes of *science* books; R = major classes of books on *medicine*. Comparable Dewey classes include: 500 Science, 590 Zoology, 600 Applied Science, 610 Medicine.

More specifically, the student might focus on such typical Library of Congress classes as:

Q   Science (General)
   QD   Chemistry
      321 Carbohydrate

QM Human Anatomy
    178 Vascular system
    404 Kidneys
    451 Nervous system
QP Physiology
    91 Blood
    111 Heart, blood vessels
    177 Relation of oxygen to metabolism
    301 General works (including physiology of exercise)
    321 Muscle
    331 Nerve
R Medicine (General)
  RM Therapeutics, Pharmacology
    221 Diets to control weight
    725 Exercise
    737 Other physiological therapy
Z Bibliography and Library Science
    5001–8000 Subject bibliography
    (Scientific subjects arranged in alphabetical sequence
    e.g., 6662 Anatomy and physiology)

For details concerning the inclusion of specific subject matter areas in the Q, R, and Z classes, the reader is directed to the following publications of the Library of Congress, Processing Department, Subject Cataloging Division:

Classification, Class Q, Science
Classification, Class R, Medicine
Classification, Class Z, Bibliography and Library Science

While major attention can be given to the Q, R, and Z classes, the reader might also note that class HB contains information on actuarial studies of build versus blood pressure and that class TX, Domestic Science, includes nutrition.

Periodicals are listed alphabetically by title in the author-title sections of the catalog files.

On numerous campuses, periodicals are listed in a separate publication which is given wide distribution, i.e., copies of *Journal and Serial Holdings* catalogs are usually located in all departmental offices and frequently appear on all graduate faculty desks. These catalogs also appear in such strategic locations as information, circulation, or reference desks of main or departmental libraries.

Periodicals such as the *Journal of Applied Physiology* or *Arbeitsphysiologie* (official title: *Internationale Zeitschrift für Angewandte Physiologie einschließlich Arbeitsphysiologie*) may be found in several departmental as well as main or divisional libraries. The exact location of these typical periodicals is ascertained following the perusal of the *Journal and Serial Holdings* catalog.

Cumulative Index Medicus,[6]* *Biological Abstracts*,[3] *Chemical Abstracts*,[5] and *Current List of Medical Literature*[7] are also useful publications.

In addition, the detailed and well documented *Physiological Reviews*,[12] *Annual Review of Biochemistry*,[1] and *Annual Review of Physiology*[2] serve as excellent sources for a sound beginning to any paper or report.

While incomplete, the following list of periodicals, including several indices, serves to illustrate the extent of information which is applicable to an understanding of human performance:

LIST OF JOURNALS

Acta Anatomica
Acta Anatomica, Supplementum
Acta Biochimica Polonica
Acta Biologica
Acta Chemica Scandinavica
Acta Chimica
Acta Endocrinologica
Acta Endocrinologica, Supplementum
Acta Physiologica Latinoamericana
Acta Physiologica Scandinavica
Acta Physiologica Scandinavica, Supplementum
Advances in Biological and Medical Physics
Advances in Biology of Skin
Advances in Carbohydrate Chemistry
Advances in Comparative Physiology and Biochemistry
Advances in Enzyme Regulation
Advances in Enzymology
Advances in Lipid Research
Advances in Metabolic Disorders
Advances in Organic Chemistry
Advances in Physical Organic Chemistry
Akademia Nauk SSSR. Doklady. Physical Chemistry (Translation)
American Dietetic Association, Journal
American Industrial Hygiene Association, Journal
American Journal of Clinical Nutrition
American Journal of Diseases of Children
American Journal of Medical Technology
American Journal of Obstetrics and Gynecology
American Journal of Physics
American Journal of Physiology

---

* *Cumulative Index Medicus* was preceded by the *Quarterly Cumulative Index Medicus*[13] (1927–1956) which, in turn, had been united with the *Index Medicus*[10] (in 1926).

American Journal of Public Health and the Nation's Health
American Journal of Science
American Journal of the Medical Sciences
American Men of Science
American Physical Society Bulletin
American Review of Respiratory Diseases
American Scientist
Anatomical Record
Annual Review of Biochemistry
Annual Review of Physiology
Applied Scientific Research, Section A. Mechanics, Heat, Mathematics
Applied Scientific Research, Section B. Electrophysics, Acoustics
Archives of Biochemistry and Biophysics
Australian Journal of Experimental Biology and Medical Science
Australian Journal of Science
Biochemical Journal
Biochemical Pharmacology
Biochemical Preparations
Biochemische Zeitschrift
Biochemistry
Biochemistry (Exerpta Medica)
Biomechanics
Biotechnology and Bioengineering
Blood, The Journal of Hematology
British Journal of Nutrition
British Medical Bulletin
Bulletin of Experimental Biology and Medicine
Canadian Journal of Biochemistry
Canadian Journal of Public Health
Canadian Journal of Research, Section E Medical Sciences
Canadian Medical Association, Journal
Carbohydrate Research
Ciba Symposia
Circulation Research
Circulation Research, Supplement
Clinical Medicine
Comparative Biochemistry and Physiology
Danske Videnskabernes Selskab, Copenhagen, Biologiske Skrifier
Diabetes
Electronic Technology
Electronics
Endocrinologia Japonica
Endocrinology
Endokrinologie
Ergonomics
Experimental Brain Research
Experimental Cell Research
Experimental Cell Research, Supplement
Gas Chromatography Abstracts
Gazzetta Chimica Italiana
General and Comparative Endocrinology

General and Comparative Endocrinology, Supplement
Giornale di Biochimica
Harvard University, Books in Biophysics
Harvey Society, New York, Harvey Lectures
Health Laboratory Science
Health Physics
Human Factors
Index Chemicus
Indian Journal of Medical Research
International Review of Neurobiology
International Zeitschrift für Angewandte Physiologie einschlieblich
    Arbeitsphysiologie
J A M A, The Journal of the American Medical Association
Japanese Journal of Applied Physics
Japanese Journal of Experimental Medicine
Japanese Journal of Physiology
Journal of Applied Chemistry
Journal of Applied Physics
Journal of Biochemistry
Journal of Biological Chemistry
Journal of Comparative and Physiological Psychology
Journal of Comparative Neurology
Journal of Endocrinology
Journal of Experimental Medicine
Journal of Food Science
Journal of Gas Chromatography
Journal of Lipid Research
Journal of Medical Education
Journal of Neurophysiology
Journal of Nutrition
Journal of Physiology
Journal of Sports Medicine and Physical Fitness
Lancet
Life Sciences
Medicina Sportiva
Metabolism, Clinical and Experimental
Methods in Enzymology
Methods of Biochemical Analysis
National Academy of Science, Proceedings
Nature (London)
Neurology
New England Journal of Medicine
New York Academy of Medicine, Bulletin
Nutrition Reviews
Perceptual and Motor Skills
Pharmacological Reviews
Physics Today
Physiochemistry
Physiological Reviews
Physiology (Exerpta Medica)
Pure and Applied Physics

Quarterly Journal of Experimental Physiology and Cognate Medical
Science
Research Quarterly
Respiration Physiology
Review of Scientific Instruments
Ricerca Scientifica
Royal Society of Edinburgh, Proceedings
Royal Society of Edinburgh, Transactions
Royal Society of London, Philosophical Transactions, Series B
Royal Society of London, Proceedings, Series B
Science
Science Abstracts
Science and Medicine in Sports
Scientific American
Societa Italiana di Scienze Naturali, Milan
Societe Française de Physiologie Vegetale, Bulletin
Society for Developmental Biology, Symposium
Society for Experimental Biology (British)
Society for Experimental Biology and Medicine, Proceedings
Society for Public Health Educators, Health Education Monographs
Yale Journal of Biology and Medicine
Vitamins and Hormones
Zeitschrift für Chemie
Zeitschrift für Physikalische Chemie (Leipzig)

Thorough familiarization with university library procedures; with interlibrary loan services; with specific location of journals, departmental and divisional libraries, duplicating or copying facilities, microtext collection, and microcard readers; and with foreign language dictionaries provides the student or researcher with the essentials for scholarly work.

A reconnaissance mission to the library is essential because it can result in more effective use of small blocks of time. Visiting the current periodicals reading room, bound periodical stacks, and book stacks and locating (and using) the card catalogs represent time well spent. When all else fails, the ever-helpful reference librarian will assist in the use of reference books and indices, and will suggest cross references.

Written Reports (Laboratory Write-Up, Term Papers)

The formats of laboratory reports vary, but usually include Title, Apparatus, Procedure, Results, Discussion, and Conclusion. Brevity must be exhibited in these reports. Completeness will be assured if the advice of Kipling is followed:

> I have six, able serving men
> They taught me all I knew
> Their names are What and Where and When
> and How and Why and Who

If these questions are answered in the report, graph, or captions to figures, an adequate story will have been told.

Given sufficient lead-time, a well-organized, well-documented term paper could be expected of each student. Note the extensive list of *periodicals* (pp. 4–7) from which the student can cite supporting data. Book authors may cite a number of foreign language articles. Should primary sources be unavailable or uncomprehended—as with certain foreign language articles—then secondary sources must be documented, e.g., "Trojonoffsky, as cited by Rich (ref. #), reported. . . ." A double-spaced, typed report is preferred. The inclusion of graphs is encouraged; they contribute to clarity as well as brevity.* Whatever their type or form, written reports must be concise, relatively free of grammatical errors, and neat. Their final form may, in fact, represent the third, fourth, even the fifth revision.

Graph Construction

Often, results can be effectively portrayed in graphic form. "One picture is worth a thousand words" is a durable saw. Yet a poorly constructed graph may be described with one word: confusing.

In order to acquire more details of graph construction, the reader is urged to consult texts such as Johnson and Jackson[11] or, for change of pace, the humorous presentation of Huff.[8] (Most assuredly, Huff points out the pitfalls of graphical presentation that must be avoided.)

All graphs are based upon a system of coordinate axes. The upper right quadrant is the one commonly used. In this quadrant, values along the ordinate begin at zero and are *positive*, while values along the abscissa, also *positive*, also begin at zero unless expressed as arbitrary units (Fig. 1–1).

Graphs, for sake of convenience and convention as well as clarity, exhibit a proportionality which is contained in such phrases as the *three-quarters rule* or the *two-thirds rule*. Thus, the ordinate, or Y axis, should be approximately three fourths or approximately two thirds of the abscissa, or X axis.

The student must also note that distances between expressed values along the ordinate are not usually the same as those along the abscissa. These distances may be equal; however, this is usually more coincidental than planned. Reducing the length of the ordinate or the length of the abscissa may be accomplished through the use of a condenser to indicate unequal divisions. In Figure 1–2, compare the distance from zero to

---

* If one accepts the statement that a graph is the equivalent of 1000 words, then it logically follows that a word is the equivalent of 0.001 graph.

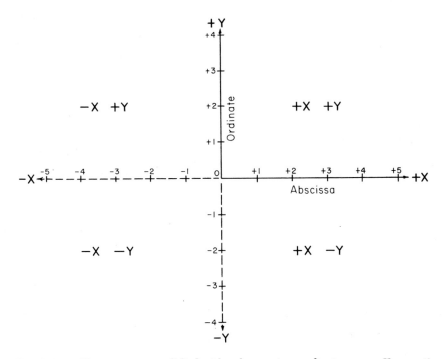

Fig. 1–1.   Plotting is accomplished with reference to coordinate axes: a Y or vertical axis (also called the ordinate) and an X or horizontal axis (also called the abscissa).

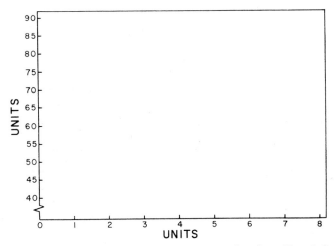

Fig. 1–2.   Distance between O and 40 on Y axis is "condensed" and depicted by condenser. Note that distances between units along X axis differ from those along Y axis.

the first numerical value to distances between succeeding values (see also Figs. 1–3A and B).

The accomplishments of several individuals or of several trials can be depicted graphically through the use of symbols which must be explained in the legend (Fig. 1–4).

Graphs which appear in most professional journals are black on white; color reproduction is expensive. It is good practice for the student also to use a black on white presentation. Rather than colored lines, the student should learn to employ symbols and varied forms of solid and broken black lines.

The final product should be neat, lettering should be large and simple in style, and units must always accompany the numerical values in Y and X axes. Labels of Y and X axes must be brief with units of measurement expressed.

The caption accompanying the figure should be descriptive and brief. Unless stated elsewhere in a laboratory report, the sex, age, height, and weight of the subject as well as the work load or type and intensity of effort should also be expressed in the caption—the "What," "Where," "When," "How," "Why," and "Who" of Rudyard Kipling's verse.

Calibration

Despite the most artistic graphical portrayal or the most robust statistical analysis, data gathered under less than exact conditions cannot withstand the test of time. Replication of studies is much in evidence in the professional literature.

Calibration involves verification through comparison of observed values to expected values. Frequency of the calibration ritual or frequency of construction of calibration curves is dependent upon the type of apparatus and frequency of the use of the apparatus as well as changing

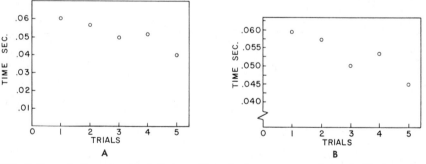

Fig. 1–3   A, Poor graphical design. Note the large space at lower half of graph. B, An improved graphical presentation. Condenser has been utilized; values along Y axis have been "spaced out."

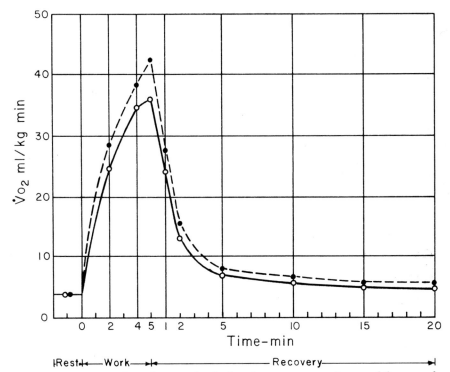

Fig. 1–4. Mean plots of two individuals. Oxygen consumption per kilogram of body weight expressed as a function of time. Note arrangement of abscissa.

atmospheric conditions such as barometric pressure or relative humidity, or great fluctuations in ambient temperature.

Verification of scale reading of a dynamometer or tensiometer is a relatively simple matter. A graded assortment of known weights is suspended from either apparatus and the scale reading noted and plotted. Mechanical adjustments should be attempted in order to rectify the discrepancy. If this is not possible, correction factors must be posted and utilized. In the interest of time economy, correction factors can usually be applied after the data have been initially recorded (see Fig. 1–5 and Table 1–1).

If wet spirometers are used, imprinted scale readings must be verified. The linear distance that the spirometer bell (or cylinder) travels is used in the calculation of volumes and subsequent verification of imprinted values.

Calibration involves the use of the formula for determining the volume of a cylinder:

$$\text{Volume} = \pi r^2 h$$
$$\text{where:} \quad \pi = 3.14159$$
$$r = \text{radius}$$
$$h = \text{vertical displacement of cylinder}$$

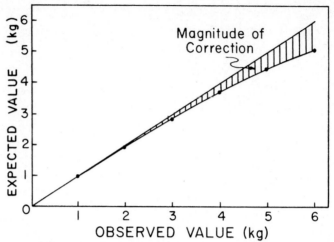

Fig. 1–5.   Graphical portrayal of discrepancy between expected or known values and observed values. Calibration of apparatus is the first order of business in experimentation. Portrayal can be in tabular form (see Table 1–1).

TABLE 1–1

EXPECTED VALUE kg	OBSERVED VALUE kg	CORRECTION FACTOR kg
1.00	1.00	+0.00
2.00	1.90	+0.10
3.00	2.80	+0.20
4.00	3.75	+0.25
5.00	4.50	+0.50
6.00	5.10	+0.90

(πr^2, which remains unchanged in each apparatus, constitutes the *bell factor* and is expressed in cc/mm—if r is expressed in millimeters. By expressing h in millimeters, volume will be expressed in cubic centimeters.)*

The discrepancy between calculated and imprinted readings is easily rectified. Suitable strips of graph paper can be utilized, or, if need be, carefully measured units etched on a strip of thin-gauge metal can be affixed over the manufacturer's readings.

Other factors, generated by mechanical design, contribute to error.

* See text page 247.

Correction factors for an unbalanced spirometer bell present a great challenge to the calibrator.

An important message that can be extracted from the above discussion favors the initial purchase of reliable equipment, rather than the continued use of inherited but inferior equipment. This does not necessarily obviate the use of cheap equipment. Rather it serves to stress the importance of prior calibration and of determining, utilizing, and reporting accuracy limits. Data must of necessity be gathered from properly calibrated apparatus.

Safety—First and Foremost

In a laboratory the probability of accident occurrence is higher than in the lecture hall. Yet, through constant reminders, strict adherence to a few "don't" rules, and the employment of proper spotting techniques, accidents can be prevented; however, *accident prevention is a full-time job.*

A few guidelines are presented:

1. The medical approval of subjects must be secured. Each individual enrolled in the laboratory section must be adjudged by competent medical authority to be capable of safely performing the laboratory exercises. In order to aid the physician, the laboratory instructor must indicate in his memorandum the nature of the laboratory experiences. The memorandum might be worded as follows:

> During the course of the semester, the following students enrolled in (course number and title or title of experiment) will be required to participate in laboratory work sessions ranging from mild to heavy. Heat-regulation mechanism, cardiovascular-pulmonary response, and metabolic demands imposed by treadmill walking and running, bicycle ergometry, stair climbing, and step testing will be observed and monitored.
>
> Please indicate those individuals who should not participate in these laboratory sessions.
>
> List students' names

2. Students should know the location of telephones in, as well as in the vicinity of, the laboratory. Conspicuously posted adjacent to the phone should be the phone numbers of (a) the director of student health or of the Campus Emergency Medical Service, (b) campus fire station, and (c) campus police station. The operator will also assist.

If the need to call arises, a brief description of the accident as well as the precise location of the laboratory must be presented.

3. Students must not sit on laboratory benches or on apparatus such as bicycle ergometers or treadmills. A treadmill which is "accidentally turned-on" might well serve as a catapult for the unsuspecting student.

Sitters on tables and laboratory benches are likely to increase the probability of contact with spilled rinsing solutions or strong acids with attendant ruined clothing and skin burns as well as the risk of toppling apparatus resulting in repair costs.

4. A spotter *must* be assigned to students engaging in any exercise. A spotter is an individual whose sole responsibility is to prevent the subject from falling but in particular to prevent the subject's head from striking the apparatus or floor. A stubbed toe resulting from an inability to maintain cadence, as in step-testing, need only result in wounded pride.

If in doubt as to proper spotting techniques, the student should ask the laboratory instructor for a demonstration.

5. When working with alternating-current electrical circuits, the beginning student must understand that there will be no trouble-shooting unless the power source is disconnected.

A sound procedure when in doubt or when "something smells hot" is to pull the plug from the 115V alternating-current receptacle.

The final step in the completion of a simple electrical circuit is connecting the plug into the power source.

6. Care must be taken in handling acids and in mixing reagents. Students will profit by reading the labels on jars containing acids or volatile solutions before using the jars' contents. *"Avoid contact with skin"* and *"Do not inhale excessively"* are two representative forms of caution that must be heeded.

When handling concentrated acids, the student will wear goggles or a face shield as well as a rubber apron. Stoppers should be replaced on all jars immediately after the desired quantity of solution or granular reagent has been removed.

Acids must be introduced slowly (and along the inside of the beaker) into aqueous solutions. To *dump* concentrated acids (dense solution) into less dense solutions is to court accident.

It is also good practice to wash and dry the hands after handling chemical solutions and reagents, especially acids.

7. All volatile solutions (such as carbon tetrachloride, acetone, and ether) should be returned to the *vented cabinet.* Under no circumstances should volatile substances be stored in a refrigerator unless the refrigerator has been de-sparked and thereby rendered explosion proof.

8. The location of the first-aid kit should be determined. In case of accident the contents of the kit must be used intelligently, and the instructor notified as soon as possible. *All accidents, however minor, must be reported to the instructor.*

9. The location and capability of the fire extinguisher should be known. The carbon dioxide extinguisher is an excellent, general-purpose type

especially recommended for extinguishing fires in electrical and electronic circuits.

10. Any cylinder containing compressed gas should be treated carefully and respectfully. Cylinders will usually be secured to a frame, base, or cart, or be chained to a table or wall; however, should any cylinder sustain a fall that shears or damages its regulator, the student must NOT attempt to prevent the escape of compressed gases by cupping a bare hand over the gas outlet. The fast flow rate of any escaping compressed gas can result in irreparable damage through tissue freezing.

Laboratories are as varied as people. Modifications of the following laboratory exercises may be necessitated by local conditions (such as apparatus availability) or as a result of emphasis desired by the instructor.

To minimize confusion, the student is urged to record in this book any departures from the plan presented.

REFERENCES

1. *Annual Review of Biochemistry.* Palo Alto, California, Stanford University Press.
2. *Annual Review of Physiology.* Palo Alto, California, American Physiological Society.
3. *Biological Abstracts.* Philadelphia, Union of American Biological Societies.
4. *Books in Print.* New York, R. R. Bowker Co. (An author-title-series index.)
5. *Chemical Abstracts.* Columbus, Ohio, American Chemical Society.
6. *Cumulative Index Medicus.* Chicago, American Medical Association.
7. *Current List of Medical Literature.* Washington, National Library of Medicine.
8. Huff, Darrell: *How to Lie with Statistics.* New York, W. W. Norton Co., 1954.
9. Hutchins, Robert M.: Personal communication, Sept. 30, 1968.
10. *Index Medicus.* Washington 1903–26. (United with the quarterly cumulative index to current medical literature to form the *Quarterly Cumulative Index Medicus.*)
11. Johnson, P. O., and Jackson, R. W. B.: *Introduction to Statistical Methods.* Englewood Cliffs, Prentice-Hall, Inc. 1953.
12. *Physiological Reviews.* Washington, American Physiological Society.
13. *Quarterly Cumulative Index Medicus.* Chicago, American Medical Association 1927–1956, superseded by *Cumulative Index Medicus.*

Chapter

2

SOMATOMETRY

A review of the anatomical landmarks cited on page 22, the reading and comprehension of pages 270–273 in *Physiological Basis of Human Performance* by B. Ricci (Philadelphia, Lea & Febiger, 1967), and the reading of Behnke[1] constitute minimum pre-laboratory preparation.

The human body exemplifies matter, for it possesses both weight and volume. The *weight* of the body is a measure of the attractive force—the pull—of the earth upon the body. *Volume* is a measure of the amount of space occupied by the body. The weight of the body mass, in fact a measure of the quantity of body solids, liquids, and gases, is a reflection of the strength of earth's gravitational attraction for the mass. For us earthlings, who at this reading are not considering bursting the bonds of the laboratory, gravitational attraction exerts a somewhat constant pull. Because of the increase in distance from the earth's center, earthlings would weigh less if the laboratory were situated at high altitude.

The quantity of solids, liquids, and gases, i.e., matter, which comprises the human frame is generally related to height. The human body is an expression of weight and volume, and weight is proportional to volume. Thus, generally expressed, a tall person will weigh more than one who is shorter. By extension, a tall adult will weigh more than a short adult, irrespective of sex. From this concept, mathematical expressions which enable one to predict weight from height have been formulated.

For example, weight expressed as a function of height may be calculated from the formula: $W_{kg} = 0.985\ H_{cm} - 100$.

If this formula were used by each member of a laboratory section and a percent error calculation applied to the results, it would be readily observed that the predictive power of the mathematical expression falls off as measures of height deviate from the mean height. The idea then is to establish the mean empirically and to establish additional deviations accordingly. Or, one might seek to ascertain the norms for all 20 year old females who are 155 cm in height. Note that two new dimensions have been added: sex and age. The formula given above could be improved if it were less general, i.e., it might be used to predict the weight of those of a particular sex and age group. Obviously, many additional formulas would be needed to predict the "ideal weight" of each sex and age group adequately.

The task of graphically portraying the relationship between height and weight for a large population would be monumental indeed; however, if it were accomplished, one would see the characteristic scatter or spread of scores with the heaviest cluster of scores falling along a straight line. To these data a regression equation could be applied and a line of best fit determined. Thus, one could then predict weight from height or predict height from weight. Obviously the latter prediction formula lacks meaning.

Mathematical formulas underlie the abundantly distributed height-weight charts. These charts have served as a semi-useful, but at the same time confusing, guide for a sizeable population; however, most of them have outlived their usefulness. Two basic reasons mitigate their effectiveness:

1. Predicting weight from one weighted factor such as height is not as powerful a technique as predicting weight from additional weighted factors (i.e., in addition to height) such as selected body diameters, circumferences, selected skinfold thicknesses, or age and sex.

2. Progeny are increasing in stature and weight. This fact serves to underscore the need for constant reexamination of the predictive power of any mathematical expression.

Height-weight charts have been used advantageously by the actuary who can present convincing argument that "overweight" individuals enjoy the dubious distinction of belonging to the high-incidence-of-mortality group.

Admittedly crude, height-weight charts nonetheless represent a low-power somatotyping method. At the opposite extreme, the densiometric technique can be utilized, thus assuring accuracy; however, financial outlay for apparatus is high.*

Between the crude and precise estimation methods cited, many techniques exist. Some involve eyeballing; others involve photographic techniques—from silhouette to photogrammetric.

In keeping with the austerity message which pervades this publication,

---

*Necessary representative apparatus includes: a large-volume water tank (into which the supine human body can be submerged), an accurate scale, a large gasometer, an oxygen tank and regulator, and a nitrogen gas analyzer. In addition, there must be provision to maintain the water temperature at 35° C.

several objective somatotype techniques requiring a small outlay of capital will be presented.

Discussion

Comparatively speaking, the fat tissue of the body possesses a lower specific gravity than does muscle tissue. Thus, the relative amounts of fat tissue to muscle tissue will be reflected in total body specific gravity.

By employing the Archimedes principle, Behnke, Feen, and Welham,[2] in 1942, determined the specific gravity of 99 naval men in the 20 to 40 year age group.

Also, in 1942 Welham and Behnke[10] presented convincing experimental evidence showing specific gravity to be an infinitely more precise index of proper weight than is weight which is based upon height. The latter index is expressed in the standard height-weight tables prepared by insurance mathematicians.

In 1945 Rathbun and Pace[9] presented a mathematical relationship in which specific gravity was used as a basis for calculating the percent of body fat.

$$\% \text{ fat} = 100 \left(\frac{5.548}{SG} - 5.044 \right)$$

This formula was revised in 1953 by Keys and Brozek[7] to account for the specific gravity of fat at body temperature.

$$\% \text{ fat} = 100 \left(\frac{5.120}{SG} - 4.684 \right)$$

Then, suggesting ". . . that the reference body, of density 1.0629 be assigned the value of 0.14 for the proportion of total fat in it," Keys and Brozek[7] proposed the following formula:

$$\% \text{ fat} = 100 \left(\frac{4.201}{SG} - 3.813 \right)$$

In 1961, Behnke[1] retained the Archimedian concept, but arrived at the assessment of lean body weight (LBW) through the use of selected body diameters and mathematical constants.

Laboratory Exercise Number 1—Estimation of Body Fat, Behnke Technique

*Required Apparatus**

Anthropometer or shoulder breadth caliper (metric units)*
Scale, physician's type, with stadiometer.

Definition of Terms

Lean body weight (LBW) as expressed by Behnke[1] is, in fact, the

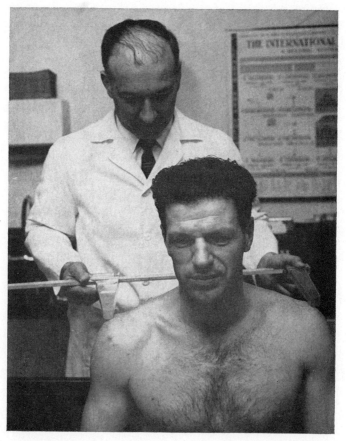

Fig. 2–1. Biacromial diameter, conveniently measured from behind, incorporates outermost projections of biacromial processes.

* For approximate cost and for suggested anthropometer source, see Appendix B, page 195.

20

weight of the lean body mass. It is the product of the mean square of body diameters divided by constants for each diameter—cm/k (LBW)— multiplied by stature (in decimeters).

$$LBW = \bar{x}^2 \times hgt_{dm}$$

Derivation of *constants* (k/LBW) was accomplished by dividing each skeletal diameter by 1.884 for reference man and by 1.719 for reference woman.

Procedure

1. Assuming the availability of a sufficient number of anthropometers, students may work in pairs or as a trio. With but one anthropometer available, many subjects can be measured if a sound organizational procedure is practiced. Obviously, the sexes must be separated. Note from the assigned reading that four measurements are taken while the subject is *seated* and the remaining measurements are taken while the subject is standing. (See Figs. 2–1 and 2–2.)

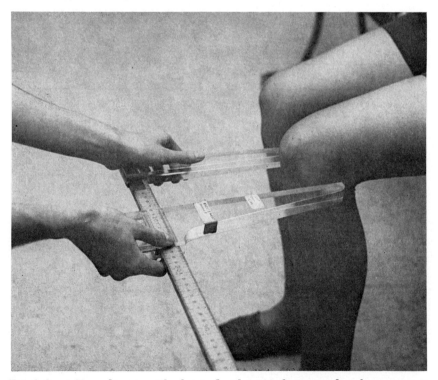

Fig. 2–2.   Knee diameter. The leg is flexed to 90 degrees and anthropometer is placed on tibiale.

An important note is in order here: all measurements, recorded in *centimeters,* must be taken with anthropometer-to-skin contact. Any intervening clothing layers will result in increases in body diameters, hence in lean body weight, and will obscure the precise anatomical landmarks thereby further contributing to error in body fat calculations.

Diameters	Constants ♂	♀
Subject in Seated Position		
Biacromial (most lateral projections of the biacromial processes are measured)	21.6	20.4
Elbow (both elbows measured; forearm fully flexed, distance between condyles of humerus measured)	7.4	6.9
Wrist (both wrists measured; measurement incorporates styloid processes of radius and ulna)	5.9	5.6
Knee (both knees measured; knee flexed to 90°; measurement is at the tibiale; medial condyle is palpable; lateral condyle measurement is immediately superior to the head of fibula)	9.8	10.3
Subject in Standing Position		
Chest (measurement taken during normal breathing at level of 5th to 6th rib space; nipple line on males)	15.9	14.8
Bi-iliac (distance between iliac crests)	15.6	16.7
Bitrochanteric (distance between most lateral projctions of trochanters)	17.4	18.6
Ankles (both ankles measured; feet spread approximately 15 cm apart, measurement taken from behind; distance between malleoli of tibia and fibula)	7.4	7.4

2. Weight (nude body) and height (without shoes) are recorded for each subject. Note that weight is expressed in kilograms while height is expressed in decimeters.

Data Treatment

1. Calculate lean body weight (LBW). Note, use eight diameters.

$$LBW = \bar{x}^2 \text{ diameters} \times hgt_{dm}$$

2. Calculate percent of body fat:

$$\% \text{ body fat} = \frac{\text{ABW} - \text{LBW}}{\text{ABW}} \times 100$$

ABW = actual body weight; LBW = lean body weight.

3. Calculate LBW by using simplified calculation procedure:

$$\text{LBW} = \left(\frac{\Sigma 8 \text{ diameters}}{101}\right)^2 \times \text{hgt}_{\text{dm}}$$

4. Proceed to calculate percent body fat.
5. Calculate LBW by using the following formula:

$$\text{LBW} = \left(\frac{\Sigma 4 \text{ diameters}}{54.8}\right)^2 \times \text{hgt}_{\text{dm}}$$

4 diameters = biacromial, bitrochanteric, both wrists, both knees

Additional Notes

The Behnke quantitative somatotype technique, involving the measurement of eight body diameters is applicable to both male and female Caucasians ranging in age from 14 to 93 years with variations in height from 15.0 to 20.0 decimeters and with variations in weight from 40 to 150 kilograms.

The accuracy of the technique is enhanced through precise measurement of the specified body diameters. Sources of measurement error are most likely in biacromial, knee, and chest diameter readings. Accuracy of chest diameter could be resolved by taking the average of maximal inhalation and maximal exhalation measurements.

More effective use of laboratory time could be attained if one person were to measure all biacromial diameters, another the elbow diameters, still another the wrists, and so on until all measurements are recorded for each subject.

The simplified calculation procedure to obtain LBW for both sexes (see 3 above) involves the summation of body diameters divided by 101, which is the summation of the constants. This procedure results in a minimization of mathematical computation at the expense of small loss of accuracy. (Note that the summation of the constants for females actually amounts to 100.7.)

The most recent suggestion of Behnke is that of using only four diameters (see 4 above). The constant 54.8 represents the summation of the constants of each of the four diameters. Behnke advocates the use of this method for "both males and females of the Caucasian and Negro races."

Discussion Topics

1. What arguments can you present for an *optimum time of day* in which to obtain all measurements necessary for the Behnke assessment of body build?

2. Speculate on the magnitude of error which can result from the chest diameter measurement. Document your answer.

3. What physiological and biomechanical arguments can you present for the adoption of standards of performance (for so-called tests of physical fitness) based upon somatotype?

4. Why is *oxygen consumption based on lean body mass* more appropriate than *oxygen consumption based on total body weight?*

Laboratory Exercise Number 2— Estimation of Body Surface Area: DuBois Height-Weight Formula

*Required Apparatus**

Scale, physician's type, with stadiometer

Definition of Terms

Body surface area, more commonly expressed in square meters, BSA_m^2, is an expression of the area occupied by the total skin surface. It is not to be confused with the area exposed to the ambient air. This latter point must be considered when discussing heat losses and gains (see text pp. 146–150).

Procedure

1. Record nude body weight, in kilograms. Leotards or tank suits may be used provided each individual wears the same type; however, possible measurement error should be noted.
2. Record standing height, in centimeters, without shoes.

Data Treatment

1. Calculate the body surface area in square meters using the modified† height-weight formula of DuBois and DuBois.[6]

(Log tables appear on pp. 190–191.)

$$A = W^{0.425} \times H^{0.725} \times 0.007184$$
$$A = BSA_m^2$$

W = body weight in kg, H = standing height in cm, 0.007184 = C = constant

SAMPLE CALCULATION: ♂ 46 yr, W = 81.72 kg, H = 175 cm

(Note: 5-place log table used)

$$BSA_m^2 = W^{0.425} \times H^{0.725} \times 0.007184$$
$$= 81.72^{0.425} \times 175^{0.725} \times 0.007184$$

Log BSA = Log $1.9123^{0.425} \times 2.2430^{0.725} \times 0.007184$
$$= .81274 + 1.62620 + \overline{3}.85637 = .29531$$

Antilog $= .29531$

BSA $= 1.973m^2$

* For approximate cost, see Appendix B, page 195.
† In the DuBois formula the constant is presented as 71.84 and the surface area is expressed in cm^2.

Compare your calculation with the figure obtained from Table 5, text page 293.

Additional Notes

The DuBois formula:

$$\text{Log. } A = \text{Log. } W \times 0.425 + \text{Log. } H \times 0.725 + \text{Log. } C \ (1.8564)$$

also referred to as the "height-weight formula," represents a simplification of the more involved "linear formula"* also devised by DuBois and DuBois.

Kleiber,[8] an eminent authority on bioenergetics, describes the DuBois formula as ". . . probably the best method of estimating the 'actual' surface area of man. It is dimensionally correct and is therefore valid for any size (as it should be)."

Body surface area data can be used to describe a subject population adequately. On the debit side, the practice of interpreting metabolic rates as a function of body surface area—$kcal/BSA_m^2/hr$—is viewed critically.

For example, Brobeck[3] points out that the dissipation of heat is not necessarily a function of skin surface area. Furthermore, changes in radiating surface areas are influenced by posture as well as microclimate.

Discussion Topics

1. Relate body surface area to heat loss and heat gain.

2. Enumerate, and document, the factors which will influence changes in body surface area.

3. List the basic conditions which must be met to ensure a valid estimation of body surface area.

4. Discuss the relative merits of describing a subject population by body surface area estimation as compared with total body density estimation.

---

* The linear formula involves measurements and constants for the head, arms, hands, trunk, thighs, legs, and feet.

Laboratory Exercise Number 3—
Estimation of Specific Gravity:
Archimedian Principle, Behnke, Feen, and
Welham Technique[2]

Required Apparatus and Materials*

Scale (autopsy type, without pan)
Scale suspension frame (see Fig. 2–3)
Weight belt (scuba accessory) (5 kg)
Scale, physician's type, with stadiometer
Spirometer, recording type, Collins (see p. 201)
Nose clip
Swimming pool equipped with 1-meter diving board (for scale suspension frame)
OR
Backyard type, above ground, circular pool, 12-gauge vinyl, of sufficient volume to contain completely submerged body

Definition of Terms

Specific gravity is defined as the ratio of the density of a substance to a standard. The standard, in this case, is water (relative density = 1.000000 g/ml at 4° C.† Refer to Table A–2 (in Appendix) for changes in specific volume of water effected by temperature. Behnke, Feen, and Welham[2] expressed specific gravity, or body density, as a ratio of body weight in air to body volume as determined by submersion.

Procedure

1. Record weight of subject attired in tank suit or trunks (see Data Sheet 2–1).
2. Subject dons weight belt and enters water *carefully* and assumes a seated position atop circular chair suspended from chain (see Fig. 2–3).
3. Following maximal inhalation, subject inserts spirometer mouthpiece then is lowered into water until completely submerged. NOTE: Subject

---

* For approximate cost and for suggested scale source, see Appendix B, pages 195–196.
† Precisely 0.999973 g/cc at 3.98° C or 1.000000 g/ml. While not applicable in this instance, the standard for gases is atmospheric air (1.000 at STP—0° C, 760 mm Hg).

Subject	Sex	A Wt kg (Air)	B Wt kg I max	C Wt kg E max	D VC L (C−B)	E Belt kg	F Gross Submerged Wt (C−E)	G Wt Loss kg (A−F)	H Gross Body Vol L	J RV L	K Net Body Vol L (H−J)	Sp. Gr. kg/L A÷K

Data Sheet 2-1

Fig. 2–3. Part of the apparatus required for weighing submerged body. Metal frame is attached to diving board. Chain was shortened to better depict circular seat.

Fig. 2–4.   A familiarization trial conducted without weight belt. Subject is breathing through tube. During actual measurement phase, spirometer would be placed on pool curb. Also, one assistant would be assigned to staff duty, i.e., staff would be lowered into water and placed within subject's reach. By this technique, a quick ascent is assured and the scale is protected against sudden jolts.

must be instructed to maintain maximal inhalation until submerged. Record weight of submerged subject at maximal inhalation.

4. While submerged, subject exhales slowly until maximal exhalation is completed. NOTE: Scale reader must monitor carefully the increase in submerged weight. Subject is likely to "reach for air" immediately after full exhalation.

5. Repeat steps 3 and 4.

Sample Calculation: ♂ 45 yrs. Letters correspond with those of Data Sheet 2–1.

A	B	C	D	E	F	G	H	J	K
81.72	6.10	9.55	3.45	4.75	4.80	76.92	76.92	1.450	75.49

$$SG = \frac{A}{K} = \frac{81.72}{75.49} = 1.082 \text{ kg/L}$$

Data Treatment

1. Calculate the specific gravity of each subject according to the following formula:

$$\text{Specific gravity kg/L} = \frac{\text{Weight, in air, kg}}{\text{Net body volume L}}$$

NOTE: Estimation of residual volume requires additional, expensive apparatus. If the apparatus is available, the calculated RV values should be used. If not, the following values are suggested:

$$\male \quad 1450 \text{ cc}$$
$$\female \quad 1250 \text{ cc}$$

With $N > 20$, Behnke, Feen, and Welham[2] selected an arbitrary figure of 1450 cc for RV for males. They state that the 1450 cc figure "will not introduce an error $\pm$ 0.003 in the computation of specific gravity."

Density is a function of water temperature. If residual volume were *measured*, densities (col. G, Data Sheet 2–1) would require corrections for water temperature. (See *Definition of Terms*.)

2. Calculate the specific gravity of each subject by using the formula of Cowgill.[5]

$$SG = 0.8 \left(\frac{H_{cm}^{0.242}}{W_g^{0.1}} \right) + 0.162$$

NOTE: Weight is expressed in grams. To compute log of weight, move decimal point one place to the left.

SAMPLE CALCULATION: $\male$ 46 yrs, W = 81.72 kg, H = 175 cm

$$SG = 0.8 \left(\frac{H_{cm}^{0.242}}{W_g^{0.1}} \right) + 0.162$$

$$= \frac{0.8 \times 175^{0.242}}{81720^{0.1}} + 0.162$$

$$= \text{Antilog } [\overline{1}.90309 + (2.24304 \times 0.242) - (4.91233 \times 0.1)] + 0.162$$

$$= \text{Antilog } [\overline{1}.90309 + 0.54282 - 0.49123] + 0.162$$

$$= \text{Antilog } [\overline{1}.95468] + 0.162$$

$$= 0.9009 + 0.162$$

$$= 1.0629^{*}$$

* Compare this body density (the author's) with the value proposed by Keys and Brozek[7] (p. 19)—proof that the author is normal.

3. Calculate the percent of body fat by employing the formula of Keys and Brozek: % fat $= 100 \left(\dfrac{4.201}{SG} - 3.813 \right)$.

4. Compare the percent of body fat for each subject estimated by the Behnke technique (text pp. 272–273) with that estimated by the Keys and Brozek formula, step 3 above. (Use densities obtained by calculation, step 1 above, and by Cowgill formula, step 2 above.)

Additional Notes

The hydrostatic principle of Archimedes which was formulated during the third century B.C. not only instigated a run in the nude to the accompaniment of "Eureka," but was to serve as a basis for the Behnke, Feen, and Welham[2] body density estimation some 23 centuries later.

A discussion of body fat estimation through specific gravity determination would be incomplete if mention of the probable sources of error were omitted. Obviously a correction for residual volume—which affects buoyancy and therefore affects the calculations—is necessary. Other sources of error include the gas volume present in the gastrointestinal tract as well as the volume of urine and feces. The effect of the latter three can be minimized through evacuation and by estimating specific gravity during the postprandial (fasting) state.

In this laboratory exercise, the maximum volume of gas exhaled following maximum inhalation (vital capacity) is monitored and therefore accounted for. Estimation of the residual volume was not accomplished. Values of 1250 cc and 1450 cc are suggested for females and males respectively.

Refinements in procedure involve the establishment of control values of one-stage vital capacity estimations for each subject in the submerged (to neck) position. In this way, maximal exhalation can be determined and compared with the values in column D, Data Sheet 2–1. Differences in values should not exceed 200 cc.

Asking subjects to exhale maximally *before* submerging constitutes an unreasonable request. Furthermore, unless the scale contains dashpots, this distressing maneuver causes wild fluctuations of scale pointer and results in guesstimation of submerged weight.

The use of the small, circular, above-ground type vinyl pool (10 feet × 30 inches) would necessitate a change of scale and body submersion apparatus. The body would be submerged in the supine position.

Discussion Topics

1. Relate specific gravity to degree of muscularity.

2. Discuss relationship between body density and energy expenditure of swimming.

3. Reconcile the difference in body fat percentages resulting from the use of Behnke and Keys-Brozek formulas.

4. Relate: weight of body fat component, percent of body fat, and lean body weight.

Concluding Remarks

Accurate estimation of body density is enhanced by appropriate apparatus (see footnote p. 18). In addition, corrections must be made for the amount of nitrogen which is present even in so-called pure oxygen. More importantly, corrections for the amount of nitrogen which is washed out of the blood and tissues (caused by decreasing P_{N_2}) must be made.

Additional somatotyping techniques are available. Some are designed for infants, others for individuals between infancy and adolescence. Still others require a substantial outlay of money for photographic equipment and supplies. These are discussed briefly in the text (pp. 270–271).

A discussion of skinfold thickness measurements has been omitted; however, the omission does not relate to apparatus cost, for skinfold calipers can be purchased for approximately $90. Rather, the variability of obtained skinfold measurements among students is of such magnitude as to question the value of a laboratory session devoted to it.

Research involving skinfold thickness measurements has been less than fruitful. The author shares the point of view well stated by Consolazio, Johnson, and Pecora[4]:

"After years of experience with measurements of skinfold thickness, the authors have come to have a very conservative attitude about them. Their limitations should be emphasized. Under controlled laboratory conditions when repetitive measurements can be made by the same observer, they may correlate with some experimental factor. For population studies by different observers, the authors question whether they do in fact correlate with nutritional status. Two major limitations have been identified:

"1. The differences between different observers measuring the same subject are extreme. Coefficients of variation of as much as 50 per cent have been found between different trained observers.
"2. The turgor of the skin is of the utmost importance. Simple dehydration will increase the skinfold thickness by as much as 15 per cent.

"In view of these limitations, the authors make the following recommendations to those using skinfold thickness measurements:

"1. All measurements should be made by a single observer who has had practice with the measuring technique for several weeks preceding the study.
"2. All measurements should be made in the early morning upon arising, in order to minimize the effect of variation in state of hydration.
"3. The measurements should be made as rapidly as possible while a scribe records the values, the series of 16 measurements on each man requiring about $2\frac{1}{2}$ min. Duplicate measurements are made

at each site before moving to the next site. The technique of measurement is completely repeated for each measurement, including regrasping of the skinfold. An effort should be made to measure the same point at each site.

"4. Since, in practical use, the skinfold measurement is converted into an index of obesity-leanness by the application of empirically derived factors, extreme conservatism should be used in interpretation."

Readers who are interested in a treatise on skinfold measurements should also refer to Keys and Brozek.[7]

REFERENCES

1. Behnke, A. R.: Quantitative assessment of body build. *J. Appl. Physiol.*, *16*:960–968, 1961.

2. Behnke, A. R., Feen, B. G., and Welham, W. C.: The specific gravity of healthy men. Body weight ÷ volume as an index of obesity. *J.A.M.A.*, *118*:495–498, 1942.

3. Brobeck, J. R.: Intermediary metabolism. *In* Ruch, T. C., and Fulton, J. F. (Eds.): *Medical Physiology and Biophysics,* 18th Ed. Philadelphia, W. B. Saunders Co., 1961.

4. Consolazio, C. F., Johnson, R. E., and Pecora, L. J.: *Physiological Measurements of Metabolic Functions in Man.* New York, McGraw-Hill Book Co., 1963.

5. Cowgill, G. R.: A formula for estimating the specific gravity of the human body with a consideration of its possible uses. *Amer. J. Clin. Nutr.*, *5*:601–611, 1957.

6. DuBois, D., and DuBois, E. F.: A formula to estimate the approximate surface area if height and weight be known. *Arch. Int. Med.*, *17*:863–871, 1916.

7. Keys, A., and Brozek, J.: Body fat in adult man. *Physiol. Rev.*, *33*:245–325, 1953.

8. Kleiber, M.: *The Fire of Life. An Introduction to Animal Energetics.* New York, John Wiley & Sons, Inc., 1961.

9. Rathbun, E. N., and Pace, N.: Studies on body composition. I. The determination of total body fat by means of the body specific gravity. *J. Biol. Chem.*, *158*:667–676, 1945.

10. Welham, W. C., and Behnke, A. R.: The specific gravity of healthy men. Body weight ÷ volume and other physical characteristics of exceptional athletes and of naval personnel. *J.A.M.A.*, *118*:498–501, 1942.

Chapter

3

CARDIAC PERFORMANCE AND RESPONSE TO EXERCISE

Preparation for this laboratory session requires the comprehension of Chapter 5, *Cardiovascular Dynamics*, in *Physiological Basis of Human Performance* by B. Ricci (Philadelphia, Lea & Febiger, 1967) as well as the pages cited in the ensuing discussion.

Fist-sized, muscular, and weighing between 350 to 500 grams, the human heart serves the indispensable function of delivering oxygen to trillions of cells having an accumulative, representative weight of 100,000 grams. Approximately 6 liters of blood are propelled through an extensive vascular bed; all cells are served oxygen and nutrients in exchange for carbon dioxide and other end products of metabolism.

In this age of heart transplantation, journalistic license has resulted in references to the heart as being "merely a pump." "Merely" is disturbing, for it suggests simplicity. In comparison to the heart, what "other pump" displays autorhythmicity, comparable endurance, and sensitivity to chemical changes in the fluid which courses through it? What "other pump" possesses the ability to chemically synthesize specific end products of metabolism in order to assure itself continued performance?

The heart is a muscular organ which lends credence to the biological dictum: function makes structure.

Because the frequency of the heart can be easily monitored, much data have been accumulated. Usually, tests of cardiovascular and cardio-pulmonary fitness include the assessment of cardiac frequency or pulse rate. Yet, cardiac appraisal which includes only cardiac frequency or pulse frequency measurements is a weak method of appraisal.

Conflicting data serve to underscore the need for additional research. Do pre-exercise pulse rates have an important bearing on post-exercise values? To cite the celebrated Harvard step-test as an example, research-ers have reported conflicting results.

Of much greater importance, however, is the recognition that cardiac frequency is but *one* factor involved in assessing cardiac performance. Of ultimate concern and importance is the knowledge of the output of the heart per unit time. It is difficult to measure stroke volume accurately; therefore, this assessment does not lend itself to extensive field trials.

Since this is a mathematical relationship, the product cannot be com-puted without knowledge of *both* values.

$$\text{Cardiac output} = \text{frequency} \times \text{stroke volume}$$

Many factors are known to affect cardiac frequency. *Emotional factors,* for example, would be a convenient title under which to group many con-tributing factors. Emotional factors trigger biochemical reactions. Is car-diac frequency, during light and moderate work loads, a true reflection of cardiac response to work? Can it also be a reflection of an individual's emotional adjustment to work?

Obviously, many questions are more easily raised than answered. Some answers lie in sophisticated research* which, by its very nature, can and should be conducted only in a medical research laboratory.† This is not to suggest that cardiac response cannot be appraised. It can. Most im-portant, however, is the awareness of results which reflect a lack of ex-perimental controls.

Blood pressure, cardiac frequency, and a general estimation of cardiac output and stroke volume can be assessed within stated limits of ac-curacy. These estimations are discussed in this section.

Discussion

Blood pressure, indirectly measured, is expressed in millimeters of mer-cury units (mm Hg). Commonly used in the assessment of blood pres-sure is the mercurial type sphygmomanometer (mercury manometer). An anaeroid‡ type of sphygmomanometer is also available. This operates on the principle of pressure differential exerted on opposing surfaces of a membrane, usually metal. A rubber membrane can also be used. (The inner surface of the metal membrane constitutes part of a metal compart-ment from which air has been removed.) The dial is calibrated in mm Hg equivalent units.

* Assessment of cardiac output *during work.*

† Special reference is made to methods based on the direct application of the Fick principle, or of such physical methods as x-ray measurement, or ballistocardiography. Indicator dilution methods, including such foreign gases as nitrous oxide or acetylene as well as intravenous injection of dyes, are subject to error.

‡ Anaeroid (without liquid, or dry type).

Substances other than mercury can be used, and in the assessment of *venous* pressure, water serves as an excellent substitute; however, for precise measurement of venous pressure, strain gauges are used to greatest advantage.

Mercury serves as an excellent substance in sphygmomanometers because it possesses a high specific gravity. Being approximately 13.6 times heavier than water, mercury allows for compactness of apparatus design. A column of mercury approximately 26.5 cm in height* is adequate for the assessment of systolic blood pressure up to 260 mm Hg.

Although weight of mercury permits compactness of design, it also serves as a variable source of measurement error. In an attempt to minimize error, the rate of air release from the inflated cuff encircling the arm should be regulated so that the resulting mercury column-drop will not exceed 3 mm/sec.

A reaction time error is unavoidably built into the reading: The reader must detect the onset of systole (and later, diastole) of the heart, then note the level of the mercury column. It is usually assumed that these errors of measurement are randomly distributed. It might be well to digress here to note that the assessment of an individual's readings though inaccurately low, or high, may correlate well with the readings by another individual. Thus, the mere computation of a high coefficient of correlation, and subsequent tests of significance, do not necessarily reflect on the competence of an individual. These results are, in fact, devoid of interpretation. What is essential is a comparison of the readings by an individual to a *standard*, i.e., to readings acquired by one whose competence is honed by experience, or, preferably, to the results acquired by a sophisticated electronic monitoring device such as a pressure transducer-recorder. (See Henschel et al.[7])

Other sources of error in blood pressure assessment may be attributed to auditory acuity and may be compounded by the transmission qualities of the stethoscope (see Ertel et al.[6]) as well as by the distraction caused by myriad noises in the laboratory. An additional source of error might be attributed to parallax; hence, the operator must position himself so that his eyes are on a level with the meniscus of the mercury column. The density of tissue layer in the antecubital space may also contribute to the possibility of error.

This enumeration of error sources, although not complete, is sufficiently lengthy to convince the reader that blood pressure measurements involving the auscultatory method (Korotkov) yield a degree of accuracy within limits. These limits must be reported. Henschel and co-workers[7] presented convincing evidence of the unreliability of the auscultatory meth-

---

* Inside diameter of tubing is 0.5 cm.

od in the determination of blood pressure. They reported that, "During standing and work the systolic pressure was underestimated by the indirect method by mean values of 8–15 mm Hg. During the first 3 min. of recovery, this method overestimated the systolic blood pressure by mean values of 16–38 mm Hg. During the hardest work level, walking at 3.5 mph on a 10% grade and during the 1st minute of recovery, a number of subjects were found in whom reasonable values for diastolic pressure could not be determined by the indirect method."

It is axiomatic that, during life, arterial blood pressure exists wherever functioning arteries exist. Thus, it is possible to wrap an inflatable type cuff at any location on an upper or lower limb. Fluids, including blood, exert pressures (Pascal's first and third laws), thus pressure values taken at any level must be corrected to heart level.* The antecubital space of the left arm affords the ideal location: it is at heart level and is accessible. The reader is reminded that blood pressure values obtained by the Korotkov technique (sphygmomanometer-stethoscope) are *approximate*.

As stated in the introduction to this chapter, precise assessment of cardiac output in man, using methods based on the direct application of the Fick principle, should be conducted only in a medical research laboratory. The reason is so obvious as to make additional discussion unnecessary. Physical methods require expensive apparatus; indicator dilution methods are subject to error.

For purposes of approximation only, and to provide the student with data which can strengthen the learning process, the utilization of the modified Fick principle is encouraged. From values provided in Table 11–5, page 267 of the text, cardiac output can be approximated from oxygen uptake values.

$$\text{Cardiac output} = \frac{\dot{V}_{O_2} \text{ ml/min}}{\text{A--V}_{O_2} \text{ diff (ml/ml)}}$$

By rearrangement of the formula—$MV = f \times SV$—stroke volume can be estimated.

$$SV = \frac{MV}{f/\text{min}} = \frac{\text{Cardiac output/min}}{\text{freq./min}}$$

* See text pages 83, 85–88, and 283–284 (Pascal's laws).

Laboratory Exercise Number 4—Estimation of Systolic and Diastolic Blood Pressure and the Recording and Demonstration of Variability of Cardiac Frequency and Pulse Rate

Required Apparatus*

Stethoscope
Sphygmomanometer, mercurial type (quick release coupling is advocated between inflatable bag and inflating bulb)
Plinth
Electric wall clock with sweep-second hand (12″ diameter dial)

Definition of Terms

The unit of measurement associated with the mercurial type of sphygmomanometer is stated in millimeters of mercury (mm Hg).

Two pressures are, by now, household terms: systolic pressure and diastolic pressure. From these readings, pulse pressure is easily obtained. Through the employment of the Korotkov technique, the measurement of *systolic blood pressure* is an estimation of the contraction of the heart, notably the left ventricle. The pressure is a reflection of the contraction of the brachial artery following its distention created by the pulse wave.† This pressure, generated by the force of arterial blood, vibrates the stethoscope diaphragm, as air from the cuff is slowly released, the pressure is transmitted as air waves through the stethoscope, and is detected as a faint "thump" sound. Upon recognition of the first sound, the operator must immediately note the level of the mercury column.

To the trained ear, a number of sounds are detectable as the cuff pressure is reduced however, unmistakable is the increase in intensity of sound level until, suddenly, the sound disappears. Precisely at this time (disappearance of sound) notation should be made of the height of the mercury column for this is an indication of diastolic blood pressure. *Diastolic blood pressure,* then, is the measure of the dilatation of the atria and ventricles of the heart as reflected by the dilatation of the brachial artery.

Freely flowing blood is not detectable with the aid of a stethoscope.

---

* For approximate cost, see Appendix B, p. 196.
† See text pages 84–85, "Maintenance of Even Flow Rates" (Borelli principle) and "Pressure Gradients."

Procedure

1. Subject is asked to assume a sitting or standing position. Record systolic and diastolic blood pressures. In addition, record pulse rate (palpation of radial artery at wrist) and cardiac frequency (stethoscope over left third intercostal space at midclavicular line) *for one full minute.* Each measure must be taken by a different person and recorded on index cards. *Comparison of results must be discouraged until all data for the complete lab session are gathered.*

If difficulty is experienced in obtaining the systolic reading, the subject should be asked to run-in-place for approximately 30 seconds. This simple exercise will be sufficient to elevate the blood pressure, thus enabling the recorder to identify the appropriate sound more easily.

Repeat roles until each student has served as subject. It is imperative that the technique of blood pressure measurements be mastered, and that these measurements be obtained within a time interval not to exceed 10 seconds per systolic measure and 10 seconds per diastolic measure. The systolic measure is decidedly more difficult to obtain than is the diastolic measure.

NOTE: Do *not* inflate cuff *over* stethoscope head. This practice is unnecessary, is uncomfortable to the subject, and may prove to be injurious to the recorder's ears during the performance of the Hyman quick standing maneuver.

2. Having mastered the techniques of assessing blood pressure and of recording cardiac frequency and radial (or carotid) pulse rate, the student is now ready to establish control values for each of these measures. The procedure must allow for a standardized position and interval of time.

A. Subject assumes a sitting position for five minutes, following which pulse rate and cardiac frequency are to be monitored and recorded for one full minute, i.e., from the fifth to sixth minute.

B. Instruct subject to think about an exciting event, or, perhaps, engage the student in a game of mental mathematics. (Ask subject to multiply—without writing materials—pairs of double digit figures, e.g., 79×24, 39×93, etc.). A three-minute work interval is suggested.

C. Immediately upon completion of step B above, record pulse rate and cardiac rate/minute. For this step, the person assigned to assess pulse rate is asked to turn his back to the clock and to count aloud (but not so loud as to disturb the individual recording cardiac rate). The individual serving as timer-recorder will jot down the pulse rate attained at the 15-second, 20-second, and 30-second marks in addition to the minute total. (See Data Sheet, 3–1.)

D. Repeat procedure until each student has served as subject.

Subject (indicate sex)	Post 5 min. Sitting Rest		Problem Solving Mental Mathematics						
	Cardiac freq/min	Radial Pulse freq/min	Cardiac freq/min	Radial Pulse					
				15"	X4	20"	X3	30"	X2	60"
1. ___									
2. ___									
3. ___									
4. ___									
5. ___									
n. ___									

Data Sheet 3-1

Data Treatment

1. Compare each adjusted pulse rate reading with the full minute reading. Calculate the percentage of error. NOTE: An adjusted pulse rate is one in which frequency is counted for a specified number of seconds and is converted to a one minute value, e.g., frequency 15 seconds $\times$ 4.

$$\text{Percent error} = \frac{\text{Difference between experimental and accepted value}}{\text{Accepted value}} \times 100$$

or

$$\text{Percent error} = \frac{\text{PR adjusted to one min—one min PR}}{\text{One min PR}} \times 100$$

2. Separate data according to sex, then calculate the mean percentage error for each of the adjusted readings.

3. Calculate the coefficient of correlation between full minute pulse rate readings (dependent variable) and each adjusted reading (independent variable).

Additional Notes

As a variable to be observed in research, cardiac frequency is preferred to pulse rate. In addition, data acquired through the use of cardiac tachometers or telemetry units are by far more valid than those gained by manual counting. When available, such monitoring apparatus should be utilized by the student.

As was previously indicated, pulse rate is an indication of the frequency of rhythmical dilatation of an artery.* Because of inter-individual

* The presence of venous pulse is recognized; however, this discussion is confined to arterial pulse, notably radial pulse.

differences in pressure, pulse rates are more easily obtained (manually) from some individuals than from others. Of importance to the reader should be the recognition of the *variability* of pulse rate (or cardiac frequency) due to psychogenic factors.

The student is directed to the text for a discussion of the factors affecting pulse rate.

Discussion Topics

1. List and comment on the possible contributory causes to an increased pulse rate.

2. Since cardiac frequency represents but *one* of two factors relating to cardiac output, what critical arguments can you present for its continued use as an indicator of cardiac fitness?

3. Discuss the merits and deficiences of recording pulse rate for 15 seconds versus the full minute count.

4. Relate the Borelli principle, elastic properties of arteries, and kinetic energy to pulse rate.

Laboratory Exercise Number 5—The Hyman Index: An Index of the Adjustment Capability of the Heart

(See text pp. 269–270)

Required Apparatus

This is the same as that required for Laboratory Exercise Number 4.

Definition of Terms

Read previous *Definition of Terms* (p. 39).

Pulse pressure is the mathematical difference between systolic and diastolic blood pressure readings.

The attention of the reader is directed to the discussion of the Hyman index (text pp. 269–270). Also the reader is urged to comprehend the difference between *mean blood pressure* (see footnote p. 269) and *average blood pressure* (obtained by merely dividing pulse pressure by two).

Procedure

1. Subject assumes a supine position, on a plinth, for three minutes. Systolic and diastolic blood pressures are recorded.

2. Subject quickly assumes a standing position (on floor). Again, systolic and diastolic pressures are recorded.

NOTE: In steps 1 and 2, systolic and diastolic blood pressures must be recorded within 10 seconds.

The services of a third person to raise and hold the sphygmomanometer at heart level will ensure more accurate results and will safeguard the sphygmomanometer when the subject assumes a standing position. The use of a wall-mounted sphygmomanometer, with tubing extension, will eliminate the need for a third person.

Data Treatment

1. Calculate the recumbent mean blood pressure index, RMBPI, using the values obtained in procedural step 1 above.

2. Calculate the quick-standing mean blood pressure index, QSMBPI, using the values obtained in procedural step 2 above.

3. Calculate the Hyman index or postural mean blood pressure index, PMBPI, then convert this value to a percentage figure.

4. Depict the data for the class in graphical form: Hyman index (Y

axis) as a function of weight* (X axis). Depict males by a black dot and females by an X.

Additional Notes

For research purposes, accuracy of readings of the *Hyman index* is assured through the use of costly apparatus. Particular reference is made to blood pressure assessment. Expensive apparatus is commercially available for the recording of blood pressures; however, existing apparatus may be modified.

Further refinements for Hyman index administration include the use of a tilt table which assures a rapid, controlled change of position from supine to erect.

Discussion Topics

1. Relate cardiac role in postural hypotensive syndrome.
2. Discuss the Hyman index in terms of hemodynamics.
3. Why must the quick-standing readings be taken within 10 seconds?
4. What is the rationale behind using mean blood pressure rather than average blood pressure? Relate these pressures to the events of the cardiac cycle.

---

* Variability in weight is assured; however, if the age of the laboratory population is varied or if percentages of body fat data are available these values may be expressed along the abscissa.

Laboratory Exercise Number 6—The Carlson Fatigue Curve Test[4]

Required Apparatus

Electric wall clock with sweep-second hand.

Definition of Terms

The Carlson fatigue curve test[4] is graphically portrayed as a fatigue curve. An *inning* is defined as the completion of a 10-second run-in-place followed by a 10-second rest interval. *Production* is a measure of the number of right-foot or left-foot contacts.

Procedure

1. For the Carlson fatigue curve test, students work in groups of three: one serves as subject, another as timer, and the third as production counter. To make foot contact more audible and thereby facilitate production count, subject may remove one shoe and engage in spot running "as fast as possible." The number of single-foot contacts is counted.

2. Record full minute, pre-exercise radial pulse rate (standing position).

3. Timer's commands are "start" and "stop." Each command is punctuated by a 10-second interval. A 10-second run followed by a 10-second rest constitutes an inning. Involved in this test is the completion of 10 full innings.

Upon completion of the test, the subject remains in a standing position and his radial pulse rates are counted and recorded from

> 10 seconds to 1 minute and 10 seconds
> 2nd to 3d minute
> 4th to 5th minute
> 6th to 7th minute

Data Treatment

1. Each student is asked to plot his own results of the Carlson fatigue curve test: production (ordinate) as a function of innings (abscissa). The name of test, initials and sex of the subject, and the date of performance should be indicated.

2. Calculate the mean and standard deviation of production per inning for the males, then, for the females. Use ungrouped data formulas for computation of mean and standard deviation. Plot production (Y axis)

as a function of inning (X axis). Use contrasting symbols to differentiate the sexes.

3. Plot pulse rates on graph.

Additional Notes

Counting the number of single-foot contacts is demanding and is subject to error due to speed of movement. Modification of the test might involve the raising of the legs until each thigh becomes parallel with the floor, thereby decreasing speed of movement and thus facilitating the production counting process. An adjustable frame can be used to ensure uniformity of thigh excursion.

A tape recorder serves to ensure accuracy of production assessment. The pick-up microphone is placed on the floor and the tape speed set at 7.5 inches/second. By playing-back the tape at 3.75 inches/second the number of single-foot contacts is easily and accurately obtained.

Maximum effort in the performance of the Carlson test is observable as a *decrease* in the slope of the curve from innings one through ten. Subsequent performances of the test will result in a raising of the curve (increase in production) but with the characteristic slope as evidence of fatigue.

Discussion Topics

1. Using recovery pulse rates as an indication of the intensity of effort, would you rate the Carlson fatigue curve test as a mild, moderate, or severe exercise? Document your answer.

2. Discuss the merits of computing "percent of application" (Carlson's term).

3. To what extent is motivation structured into the Carlson test?

4. What effect would reducing production (by raising each leg until the thigh is parallel with the floor) have on energy expenditure? Why?

Laboratory Exercise Number 7—Cardiac Adjustment to Change in Rate and Amount of Work

*Required Apparatus**

2 benches; one 20.3 cm in height; one 40.6 cm in height. Both benches 2 meters in length and 30.5 cm in width
1 Electric metronome (40–208 strokes/min)
1 Stethoscope
1 Electric wall clock with sweep-second hand
1 Scale, physician's type with stadiometer

Definition of Terms

Work, defined as the product of force acting on a mass through a distance, is affected by many factors including inertia to be overcome, speed of contraction or rate of work, duration of effort, environmental conditions, somatotype, and numerous other physiological and psychophysiological factors.

Differentiation is made between positive and negative phases of work. Positive work is accomplished in opposition to a resistive force including gravitational force. *Negative work* is accomplished with assistance from force.

Procedure

1. Weight of subject is recorded (in kg).
2. Subject is asked to assume a sitting resting position for five minutes. Record cardiac frequency (stethoscope head placed over the intercostal space of left third rib at mid-clavicular line) for *one full minute.*

In coeducational situations, radial pulse frequency may be substituted; however, count is to be taken for *one full minute.*

3. Subject engages in step testing on the 20.3-cm bench at the rate of 16 completed steps per minute (metronome set at 64) for three minutes.
4. Upon completion of exercise, subject again assumes a sitting position. Post-exercise cardiac frequency (or pulse rate) is recorded from:

30 seconds	to 1 minute and 30 seconds
2 minutes	to 3 minutes
3 minutes and 30 seconds	to 4 minutes and 30 seconds
and 5 minutes	to 6 minutes

* For approximate cost, see Appendix B, page 197.

5. Upon completion of the above exercise by all subjects, each is to participate in another three-minute step-testing exercise on the 40.6-cm bench. The order of testing must remain unchanged. Cadence is maintained at 64. Cardiac frequency is monitored and recorded for the same post-exercise intervals (see 4 above).

6. Allow one-half hour rest period in the sitting position before proceeding with the third exercise: 40.6-cm bench stepping at increased cadence: 30 completed steps/minute (metronome set at 120). Maintain the same order of testing.

Cardiac frequency is monitored and recorded for the same post-exercise intervals (see 4 above).

Data Treatment

1. Calculate positive work accomplished by each subject during each exercise (see steps 3, 5, 6 of *Procedure*). (See also text pp. 261, 266–267 for calculation of work.)

2. Plot cardiac response to changes in *amount* of work—comparison of procedural steps 3 and 5—as well as cardiac response to changes in *rate* of work—comparison of procedural steps 5 and 6. Be certain to include pre-work, rest values.

Additional Notes

The message contained in paragraph one under "Additional Notes" (p. 41) is also appropriate here.

To ensure an adequate recovery between successive step-tests, the order of testing must remain unchanged.

Variations in this laboratory exercise involve the use of a treadmill and a bicycle ergometer.

1. Treadmill*
   - A. Maintain constant grade, e.g., 10%; vary belt speed, e.g., 7 km/h and 10 km/h.
   - B. Maintain constant belt speed, e.g., 6 km/h; vary grade, e.g., 4% and 8%.
2. Bicycle ergometer†
   - A. Maintain constant work load, e.g., 2 kg load on weight pan; vary frequency of pedaling, e.g., 40 rpm and 80 rpm (metronome set at 80 and 160 respectively).
   - B. Maintain constant rate of pedaling, e.g., 40 rpm; vary load on weight pan, e.g., 2 kg followed by 4 kg.

---

* See text page 261 for calculation of work on treadmill.

† See text pages 266–267 for calculation of work: kgm, kpm. See also page 289 for relationship of kpm to kgm. (Kiloponds unit of force exerted by gravity on a mass of 0.1 kg.)

For details on construction of a frictional bicycle ergometer, see Karpovich,[10] von Döblen,[15] and Howie.[8,9] Of interest to the student researcher is the use of a treadmill to drive a bicycle ergometer.[11]

Further variation in these laboratory exercises might include the use of elgons (p. 92 ff) to assess joint range of movement or the open-circuit indirect calorimetry technique to determine oxygen consumption (see p. 149). Based on oxygen consumption data, and on cardiac frequency data, cardiac output values as well as stroke volumes may be calculated (see text pp. 267–268). In addition, oxygen pulse and cardiac index may be calculated (see text pp. 268–269).

Discussion Topics

1. Relate moments of force to bench-stepping exercises.
2. Why do cardiac frequency and the pulse rate increase with exercise?
3. What effects will long limb segments have on energy expenditure?
4. Enumerate, and discuss briefly, the kineoenergetics of performance in which changes in intensity and duration of effort are introduced.

Concluding Remarks

Cardiac response to exercise, as indicated by changes in cardiac and pulse frequency, is an oft-used variable. Especially at elevated frequencies, the accuracy of the count is increased immeasurably when the human ear is replaced by the electronic ear.

Blood pressure values, obtained through the use of the auscultatory method (Korotkov), must be regarded as *approximate*. The monitoring of these variables in *research* studies must be accomplished by electronic devices.

Electrocardiograms enrich the laboratory experience. Unfortunately these tracings are beyond the reach of the individual who lacks the essential, somewhat costly apparatus. Mention is made of the ECG* because of the lengthy discussions which frequently take place at professional meetings relative to the significance or nonsignificance of the various segments. Placement of the leads is extremely important (see text pp. 101–102). Unless the leads can be placed over the identical areas during subsequent monitoring, comparison of ECG tracings lacks meaning and power.

The reader is urged to review Figure 5–9 (text p. 100) and to notice the interrelationship of the ECG tracing with the interval of systole as well as with the occurrence of the "lupp" sound. Note also the relationship of the T wave, of the ECG, to the extent of left ventricular and aortic pressures.

Discussion of physiological fitness, more especially of so-called physical fitness,† is usually spirited. Noticeable, especially in the physiological fitness tests, is the inclusion of pulse rate. On would be remiss to exclude passing reference to the Harvard step-test—the *cause célèbre*. Lowering of bench heights has been advocated by Clarke[5] and by Sloan[14] irrespective of the mechanical advantage possessed by some long-limbed women over shorter-limbed males. This has been challenged by Ricci and associates[13] and by Cairns.[3]

Early evaluation of the test was given by Bean and co-workers.[2] The test continues to be evaluated.

The Harvard step-test has been described by some subjects as "challenging" and by others as "gruelling." Nevertheless, from the researchers' point of view, the test has value.

The reader with more than casual interest in the Harvard step-test will benefit by perusing the studies cited above as well as those by Ariel[1] and by Reedy and colleagues.[12]

* ECG = EKG; EKG reflects the Germanic influence.
† See text pages 233–237.

The Harvard step-test is singled out because of its renown and its suitability to extensive use because of minimal apparatus requirements and the ease with which it may be administered.

Irrespective of the tests used, the reader must be prepared to discuss the relative merits of physiological fitness tests in which pulse rate or cardiac frequency are used in the scoring index.

REFERENCES

1. Ariel, G.: The effect of knee-joint angle on Harvard step-test performance. *Ergonomics, 12*:33–37, 1969.

2. Bean, W. B., Park, C. R., Bell, D. M., and Henderson, C. R.: A critique of physical fitness tests, Report Nr. 3: Army Medical Research Laboratory, Fort Knox, Kentucky, Feb. 19, 1947.

3. Cairns, M. A.: The effects of undiscernible changes in bench height on Harvard step-test performance of women. Unpublished Master's thesis, University of Massachusetts, 1968.

4. Carlson, H. C.: Fatigue curve test. *Res. Quart., 16*:169–175, 1945.

5. Clarke, H. L.: A functional physical fitness test for college women. *J.H.P.E.R., 14*:358–359, 394–395, 1943.

6. Ertel, P. Y., Stern, A. M., Brown, R. K., and Gillespie, D. E.: Acoustic differences among stethoscopes. *J. Univ. Michigan Med. Center, 32*:35–38, 1966.

7. Henschel, A., de la Vega, F., and Taylor, H. L.: Simultaneous direct and indirect blood pressure measurements in man at rest and work. *J. Appl. Physiol., 6*:506–508, 1954.

8. Howie, A.: "'Workshop Corner'" bicycle ergometer. *New Zeal. J. Phys. Educ., 40*:57–60, 1966.

9. ————: "'Workshop Corner'" bicycle ergometer (concluding article). *New Zeal. J. Phys. Educ., 41*:55–59, 1967.

10. Karpovich, P. V.: A frictional bicycle ergometer. *Res. Quart., 21*:210–215, 1950.

11. Lurie, P. R.: Conversion of treadmill to cycle ergometer. *J. Appl. Physiol., 19*: 152–153, 1964.

12. Reedy, J. D., and Saiger, G. L.: Evaluation of the Harvard step-test with respect to factors of weight and height, Report Nr. 140: Army Medical Research Laboratory, Fort Knox, Kentucky, June 10, 1954.

13. Ricci, B., Baldwin, K., Hakes, R., Fein, J., Sadowsky, D., Tufts, S., and Wells, C.: Energy cost and efficiency of Harvard step-test performance. *Arbeitsphysiol., 22*:125–130, 1966.

14. Sloan, A. W.: A modified Harvard step-test for women. *J. Appl. Physiol., 14*:985–986, 1959.

15. von Döblen, W.: A simple bicycle ergometer. *J. Appl. Physiol., 7*:222–224, 1954.

Chapter

4

ANALYSIS OF GROSS MUSCLE FUNCTION

Comprehension of the following is required: Chapter 2, *Muscle Considerations;* pages 31-34, 36-38, and 43-49 in Chapter 3, *Neural Control of Muscle Activity;* and Chapter 4, *Kineoenergetics* (all in *Physiological Basis of Human Performance* by B. Ricci [Philadelphia, Lea & Febiger, 1967]).

The term *strength* is indelible.

Atlas supported the heavens on his shoulders, and in modern times is depicted as supporting the earth—in strictly non-Newtonian fashion for where was his base of support? The term "atlas" is associated incongruously with handbooks on technical subjects. Atlas was overthrown by Hercules.

Hercules, son of Zeus and Alcmene, performed great feats of strength—not suprisingly, for he was, after all, the son of the supreme deity of the Greeks. We presently refer to powerful and courageous acts as displays of *herculean* effort.

Antaeus (Antaios), a mythical Greek giant, was considered to be a great wrestler who was unbeatable as long as he remained in contact with his mother, the earth. Even in modern times it is considered wise to prevent being "swept off one's feet."

The Israelites produced Samson, the strong one who was later betrayed to the Philistines by his mistress Delilah. Goliath, the gigantic Philistine, was killed by David.

Persons of great strength and courage are known as *lions,* e.g., Richard Coeur de Lion, Richard I of England, Richard the Lion-Hearted. Also there are social lions.

All of the real and fictional characters mentioned above undoubtedly possessed one common quality: they were probably thewy (muscular). Physical strength is an expression of muscle action which implies the quality of being strong, and being capable of demonstrating force, power, and vigor. Strength was once considered a virtue, but as the lexicographer points out, "the sense or term is obsolete."

Discussion

Strength is an incomplete term. As reflected in the numerous published studies of human strength, much is *implied* by its use; however, it is often diminished in interpretive power.

Force is a more precise term. By substituting force for strength in the description of human accomplishment, an author imparts to the reader a more complete expression because *force*, a vector quantity, expresses both *magnitude* and *direction*. Thus, the rope-pull coach can select his squad members scientifically by having each prospect exert a force that is measured by a dynamometer or appropriate spring balance. The selection problem is not a simple one. An analysis of the events which culminate in the Coach-of-the-Year Award would reveal the successful rope-pull coach to be one who related pulling force to body mass—a technique which yields more meaningful data. The coach strives for awesome pulling capability,* but also wishes to field a formidable mass which not only demoralizes the opponents but also metabolically weakens them into submission.

Simply expressing isometric force is not as meaningful as expressing force which is related to area of muscle tissue. Consequently, evaluation of a physical act, e.g., lifting either packages or bar-bells, is precise if the force which is required to produce motion—to move the package or bar-bells—is related to the muscle cross-sectional area† or to the lengths of the lever arms. In such total body activities, analysis is complex because precise evaluation implies consideration and calculation of free body diagrams‡ of displacement and force moments. Although *greatly diminished* in interpretive power, the exerted force in bar-bell or package lifting may be more clearly expressed per unit of body weight or, more precisely, per unit of lean body weight; however, this is not without the attendant danger of presenting misleading information. The following example

---

* It would also be learned that the coach had read the study of Ringelmann (reported by Moede and cited by Dashiell[2]) and had succeeded in reducing the coordination loss. In brief, Ringelmann's population included persons each of whom could pull an average equivalent load of 63 kg; however, two persons pulling together managed *not* 126 kg but 118 kg; a trio pulled 160 kg rather than 189 kg (63 × 3). Eight people (ideal rope-pull squad size?) cooperatively pulled 248 kg rather than 8 × 63 kg or 504 kg.

† Cross-sectional implies measurement which is perpendicular to long axis of muscle fibers.

‡ Free body diagram: a diagram depicting all forces acting on total body or body parts—forces which are linear, parallel, concurrent and resultant.

serves to clarify this point. Males A and B of similar age and height performed pull-ups on the gymnastic still rings. Vertical body displacement
(measured at the suprasternal notch) amounted to 50 cm/pull-up.

Subject	Wt (kg)	Pull-ups (pu)	pu/kg	Displacement (m)	Work (kgm)
A	50	3	.06	1.5	(50 × 1.5) = 75
B	100	6	.06	3.0	(100 × 3.0) = 300
B	100	1.5	.015	0.75	(100 × 0.75) = 75
B	100	3	.03	1.5	(100 × 1.5) = 150

Note that subject B must perform *double* the number of pull-ups to
achieve the *same* pu/kg body wt index as A achieves. Yet, when expressed
as kgm work, B's accomplishment is *four times greater* than that of A.
To attain the *same* work output, it is necessary for B (third entry) to
perform *one half* the number of pull-ups as A, which amounts to *one-
fourth* the pu/kg index.

As portrayed by the last entry, the accomplishment of equal numbers
of pull-ups (3) by persons of diametric mass (50 kg vs 100 kg) may
provide justification for three varying statements: (1) that the individuals
are *equal* in terms of pull-up accomplishment, or (2) that A is to be
ranked *higher* than B because of achieving a greater pu/kg index, or (3)
that B is to be ranked *above* A because he performed twice as much work.
This point need not be belabored. Suffice it to say that sweeping reforms
are long overdue, in fact urgently required, to translate test items of so-
called tests of "physical fitness" into expressions which consider—*not
totally disregard*—biomechanical factors.

Assessing the force capability of the quadriceps muscle group or of the
forearm flexors in phasic contraction might be accomplished with respect
to the length of the lever arm. In both of these examples, force gives way
to such precise terms as *torque* or *moment of force*. The units of measurement reflect extent of inertia and displacement as well as length of lever
arm involvement, e.g., kilogram meters or kilogram or gram centimeters.

Assessment of force capability of the above-mentioned muscle groups
during static contraction should include an analysis of the composition
and resolution of forces and should be related to muscle group cross-sectional area, e.g., force/cubic centimeter of muscle tissue.

The reader must not infer that strength cannot be used with reference
to muscle. It can. However, it is best modified by an adjective as in describing *tensile* strength of muscle tissue. In this example, the maximum

stress* which muscle tissue is capable of sustaining is expressed in relation to cross-sectional area.

In order that greatest meaning be extracted, force must be expressed relative to body mass or, when applicable, must reflect the integrative action of the muscle-skeletal systems and therefore be expressed relative to muscle cross-sectional area or to length of lever arm.

* *Stress* describes the distorting force whereas *strain* describes the distortion resulting from stress.

Laboratory Exercise Number 8—
Interrelationship of Load and Cadence to
Girth of Forearm Flexors

(Read text pp. 228–230)

*Required Apparatus and Materials**

Electric metronome (40–208 strokes/min)
Dumb bells (2 kg, 5 kg)
Electric wall clock with sweep-second hand
Gulick tape†
Plethysmograph
Skin marking pencil

Definition of Terms

Range of movement (ROM) is indicative of the extent of body segment excursion permitted by the joint; it is measured in degrees (see
pp. 91–92).

In this context, *fatigue* is defined as the inability of the subject to maintain strict cadence of forearm excursion through a prescribed range of
movement. *Duration of effort* is the elapsed time between the beginning
of the exercise bout and the manifestation of fatigue.

Work is the product of mass times the total displacement of mass. In
this laboratory exercise, only the positive aspect of work is considered.

Moment of force, or *torque,* is the product of the perpendicular force
times the length of the lever or moment arm. The moment arm is measured from the point of force application to center of joint rotation. The
terms are compatible. Torque must not be reserved solely for use in
describing a twisting motion, for torque is equally descriptive of a rotating motion. The reader will recall that the semilunar or trochlear notch
of the ulna rotates or "turns around" the trochlea of the humerus.

A *plethysmograph* is defined simply as an apparatus for measuring
volume of body organs, limbs, segments, or the whole body. Water displacement, the Archimedian concept, represents a convenient, inexpensive, and accurate method of measurement.

---

* For approximate cost and for suggested Gulick tape source, see Appendix B,
page 197.
† Spring attachment provides constant tension on the tape.

Procedure

1. Measure and record distance from medial epicondyle of humerus to mid-palm of preferred arm.

2. Flex the forearm to 90 degrees and exert maximum tension. With Gulick tape, measure circumference of arm (record in cm).

3. Determine the hand volume (see Fig. 4-1).

   A. Record initial water level in plethysmograph; record water temperature.* (See Data Sheet 4-1.)

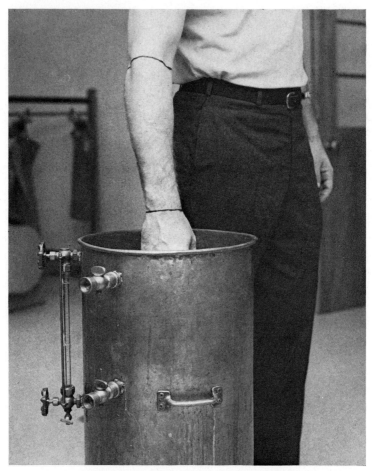

Fig. 4–1.   Plethysmograph constructed locally. Inside diameter of base = 32 cm. Plethysmograph factor (πr^2) = 804.25 ml/cm. Water displacement is noted in calibrated glass tube shown at left of apparatus. Outlines of segment limits are depicted.

* Comfort must dictate water temperature. For hand and forearm immersion, 20 to 23° C is satisfactory. Lower limb or trunk immersion usually necessitates increases in water temperature to 27° C.

Subject Sex	Segment		A Water t°C	B Initial Level mm	C Submerged Segment Level mm	D Factor* ml/mm	E Vol ml $(C_{\bar{x}})(D)$	F Water Density g/ml	G Segment Wt_g (E)(F)	H Segment Wt_{kg} G÷1000
			Plethysmograph							
A	Hand	1 2 3								
				Σ = mm						
				$\bar{X}$ = mm						
A	Fore-arm	1 2 3								
				Σ = mm						
				$\bar{X}$ = mm				**	**	

* Factor: πr^2 for plethysmograph

** For forearm subtract hand wt.

Data Sheet 4-1

B. With skin pencil, mark location of wrist joint center. Instruct subject to slowly immerse preferred hand into plethysmograph to joint center. Record water level.

C. Repeat above procedure three times.

4. Determine the hand and forearm volume; repeat steps 3A, B, and C. NOTE: Subject slowly immerses forearm to level of elbow joint center (see Fig. 4-2).

5. Subject assumes position before wall (see Fig. 4-3) and exercises at load and cadence as indicated below:

Load (kg)	Cadence (lifts/min)	Metronome Setting
2	20	40
2	40	80
5	20	40
5	40	80

For each subject, record cadence and duration of effort for each load (see Data Sheet 4-2). NOTE: Subjects must exercise in a predetermined order and all subjects must complete one load-cadence combination before proceeding to another. To reduce the influence of fatigue between successive work bouts, the order of testing must remain unchanged. The order of testing in this exercise is based on expediency. Were this a research project, an order of testing per subject which would rule out

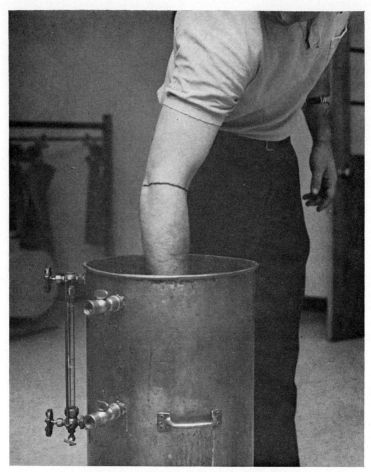

Fig. 4–2.   Measurement of hand volume. Hand is immersed to wrist level (see Fig 4–1). Note provision for water-collecting method. For leg immersion, false bottoms are utilized for ease of use and measurements.

Subject	Sex	Cadence min	Arm Circumference cm	Forearm Moment Arm cm	Load kg	Hand + Forearm wt, kg	Work kgm	Duration of Effort sec	Power kgm/sec

Data Sheet 4-2

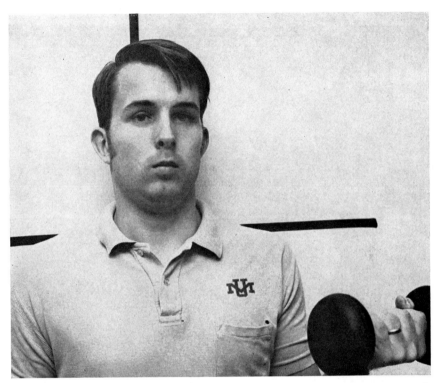

Fig. 4–3.   Plastic tape applied to wall. Subject aligns his vertebral column with vertical line and stands erect and in contact with the wall. Fatigue is exhibited when cadence cannot be maintained while keeping the body erect. Horizontal line at shoulder level serves as a reference line. Only minimal trunk bending is allowed.

possible sequence of measurements effects, i.e., from practice and learning, would take this form:

1 2 3 4
2 3 4 1
3 4 1 2
4 1 2 3
1 3 2 4
2 4 3 1
3 1 4 2
4 2 1 3
etc.

Conditions:	1	2 kg	20 lifts/min
	2	2 kg	40 lifts/min
	3	5 kg	20 lifts/min
	4	5 kg	40 lifts/min

Data Treatment

1. Calculate weight of hand and of forearm by converting volume into mass:

$$Wt = Vol \times Mean\ Density^*$$
$$= V \times \overline{D}$$

A. Weight of hand is calculated first (see Data Sheet 4-1).

$$Wt_{kg} = V_{h\ ml} \times 1.155$$

B. Calculate weight of forearm by first *subtracting* hand volume from mid-elbow immersion volume:

$$Wt_{kg} = V_{fa\ ml} \times 1.125$$

2. Calculate moment of force for each of the two load displacements.
3. Calculate work accomplished with each load at each cadence.

$$W_{kg\ cm} = F_{kg} \times S_{cm}$$
$$= load_{kg} \times \pi\ (moment\ arm_{cm})$$

NOTE: Load = weight of dumb bell *plus* combined weight of forearm and hand; $\pi = 3.1416$.

4. Calculate power for each load at each cadence; express power in kgm/sec:

$$P = \frac{W}{t}$$

5. Calculate torque in kg cm. (NOTE: Static position disregarding inertial forces.)
6. Using total group data, calculate a coefficient of correlation between arm circumference and work accomplished at each load and cadence level.
7. OPTION: Rather than calculate the coefficient of correlation, plot total group data graphically: circumference (Y axis) as a function of work (X axis) for each load and cadence level.

Additional Notes

Calculation of physical work accomplished at each load and cadence is approximate, i.e., the actual displacement of the load is *approximately* one half the circumference of a circle which is described by the load-in-

* See Table A–3, in the Appendix for mean density values for all body segments.

hand plus weight of hand and forearm. The radius of the circle is represented by the moment arm, hence justification for the use of π, or 3.1416, multiplied by the moment arm. This represents a formula simplification for displacement which is applicable to loads being moved about an established semicircular path.

$$\frac{2 \ \pi \ \times \ \text{moment arm}}{2}$$

One may justifiably and convincingly argue that an *approximate* forearm *and* hand, mean segment density value of 1.14 be utilized thus eliminating the requirement of calculating hand weight first, followed by forearm weight. If only approximate values are desired, the value 1.14 is acceptable for use. Furthermore, although it is recognized that water density is a function of water temperature (see Table A-2 in the Appendix), relative density and volume of water may be taken as 1.0000 grams/milliliter irrespective of water temperature. This practice compounds error; however, it is justifiable if *approximations* only are desired.

More sophistication can be introduced into this laboratory exercise by utilizing an elgon to monitor elbow joint range of movement (see p. 89). Fatigue of forearm flexors would be noted by a decrease in joint range of movement in order to maintain cadence or by an inability to maintain strict cadence through a prescribed range of movement. With time lines on the goniogram, cadence can be verified.

Assessment of body segment volume is accomplished with the aid of the "workhorse" formula: $V = \pi r^2 h$. (Obviously, this formula implies the use of a cylindrical plethysmograph; rectangular plethysmographs would require a formula which includes the area of the base times the height.)

A simpler, slower method of estimating segment volume involves the collecting and weighing of displaced water. This method is especially suited for use involving plethysmographs which are not cylindrical or rectangular.

Relating arm circumference to muscle force is a gross technique because circumference measurement includes bone as well as fat tissue, fascia, nerves, and blood vessels which understandably do not produce force as does muscle tissue. An alternative—that of calculating muscle cross-sectional area—does not readily lend itself to a laboratory exercise. The interested reader is urged to review the techniques of Clark[1] and the article of Morris.[7] The Clark formula for area is presented below; the measurements are those of the author (Ricci).

With forearm flexed at 90 degrees, measurements are taken from the area of greatest circumference of biceps-triceps; readings are corrected for fat. Width = 8.0 cm; depth = 11.8 cm; circumference = 33.5 cm.

$$\begin{aligned}
\text{Arm Area}_{cm^2} &= \text{width}_{cm} \times \text{depth}_{cm} - (.603553 \, [2(W + D) - \text{circumference}_{cm}])^2 \\
&= 8.0 \times 11.8 - (.603553 \, [2(8.0 + 11.8) - 33.5])^2 \\
&= 94.4 - (.603553 \, [2(19.8) - 33.5])^2 \\
&= 94.4 - (.603553 \, [39.6 - 33.5])^2 \\
&= 94.4 - (.603553 \, [6.1])^2 \\
&= 94.4 - 13.557 \\
&= 80.843_{cm^2}
\end{aligned}$$

Muscle area$_{cm^2}$ = arm area$_{cm^2}$ $\times$ average muscle proportion*
Forearm flexors:

Biceps brachii = $80.843_{cm^2} \times 0.1934 = 15.635_{cm^2}$
Brachialis   = $80.843_{cm^2} \times 0.2083 = 16.839_{cm^2}$

Forearm extensor:
Triceps brachii = $80.843_{cm^2} \times 0.4271 = 34.528_{cm^2}$

Force, i.e., flexion, extension, compression, etc., may then be clearly expressed in kg/cm².

Discussion Topics

1. Discuss the relationship between torque and muscle cross-sectional area.

2. Discuss "muscle tone." Present a chemo-electrical basis for its presence.

3. With reference to muscle group action, present a working definition of the following terms: work, power, fatigue, endurance, hypertrophy, gradation, recruitment, static, phasic.

4. Cite physiological evidence which justifies alternating rhythmical muscle contraction to static or isometric contraction. Relate to physical performance of sustained duration.

---

* From Morris.[7] The average proportion of each muscle was measured with the aid of a disc planimeter from two sets of cross-section drawings.

Laboratory Exercise Number 9—Force Analysis in Knee Extension

(Read text pp. 54–58)

*Required Apparatus and Materials**

Gulick tape†
Plethysmograph
Goniometer (plastic)
Skin-marking pencil

Definition of Terms

Reread "Definition of Terms" on pages 91–92.

Extension of the leg, a function of the vasti and rectus femoris muscles, is performed under the typical mechanical disadvantage which characterizes man. In fact, man is a collection of lever systems which associate short force arms with long resistance arms. In relation to the greater distances through which loads are moved, the muscle insertions move notably shorter distances. Through this mechanical arrangement, man has acquired not only the capability of exerting great force, but also has gained tapered limbs and slim joints which contribute to beauty of body design.

Force is manifested in the act of knee extension. At any position of the leg, force must be analyzed not only in *magnitude* but in direction—force being characterized by horizontal, vertical, and resultant components relative to the leg axis. In the sitting position (leg flexed at 90 degrees) the load‡ offers negligible resistance to leg extension; however, as the leg is moved closer to full extension, the load exerts successively greater resistance to extension.

Of particular interest is the rotary component of the load: at 90 degrees it is zero; at 180 degrees (extension) it is equal to the load and acts to rotate the leg downward to the 90-degree or vertical position. From the standpoint of quadriceps muscle involvement, greatest tension is exerted at 180-degree extension.

Procedure

1. Measure and record distance from knee joint to medial malleolus (ankle center).

---

* For approximate cost and for suggested Gulick tape source, see Appendix B, page 197.
† Spring attachment provides constant tension on the tape.
‡ Load includes weight of leg and foot.

2. From the standing position (feet spread 30 cm apart), exert maximum tension in the quadriceps muscle group of the preferred limb. With Gulick tape, measure circumference of leg at a level 16 cm above superior border of the patella.

3. Determine the combined leg and foot volume (see pp. 57–59).

    A. Record initial water level in plethysmograph; record water temperature.

    B. Instruct subject to slowly immerse preferred leg into plethysmograph to level designated by mark established in procedural step 1. Record water level.

    C. Repeat above procedure three times. NOTE: Use data sheet similar to Data sheet 4-1.

4. Subject is seated atop a sturdy table or plinth. Instruct subject to fold arms across chest, to extend leg 45 degrees from vertical, and to hold this position as long as possible. Record duration of interval. NOTE: Do not allow subject to become informed of duration of interval until step 5 is completed.

5. After all subjects have performed the preceding step, each subject will again extend the leg to 75 degrees and again hold this position as long as possible. Record duration of interval.

Data Treatment

1. Calculate weight of leg and foot by converting volume into mass:

$$\text{Wt} = \text{V} \times \overline{\text{D}}$$

$\overline{\text{D}}$ for leg and foot $= 1.09$. NOTE: This represents a departure from Dempster[3] (see Table A-3 in the Appendix), who advocated that foot and leg volumes be measured separately. (See Dempster[4] also.)

2. Calculate, algebraically, torque (the rotatory component of load): weight of leg and foot at leg extension angles of 90, 120, 135, 150, 165, and 180 degrees. Plot results graphically: percent application Y axis, theta angle X axis.

SAMPLE TORQUE CALCULATION. Given:

    wt of leg and foot 2.05 kg; leg extended to 135 degrees; leg length 40 cm

NOTE: Angle theta ($<\theta$) is formed by the leg with reference to vertical. Thus, with leg extended to 135 degrees, angle at knee joint with respect to vertical is 45 degrees. Refer to Tables A–6 and A–7 in the Appendix.

$$
\begin{aligned}
<\theta = \ & 45°, \text{ sine } = .70711 \text{ load} \\
= \ & .70711 \times 2.05 \text{ kg} \\
= \ & 1.45 \text{ kg}
\end{aligned}
$$

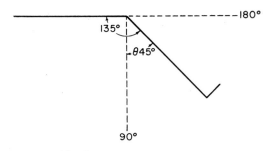

Fig. 4–4.   Component of load.

Force expressed as a percentage of total force in full extension:

$$= 1.45 \div 2.05 \times 100 = 71\%$$

Torque: Leg length 40 cm; center of gravity as a percentage of segment length, 60.6%* (from knee joint to medial malleolus)

$$= \frac{60.6}{100} \times 40 \text{ cm} = 24.24 \text{ cm}$$
$$= 1.45 \text{ kg} \times 24.24 \text{ cm}$$
$$= 35.15 \text{ kg cm}$$

3. Using total group data, plot circumference of thigh (Y axis) as a function of duration of effort (X axis). Use symbols which differentiate male from female accomplishments.

Additional Notes

Refinement can take the form of utilizing an elgon† to monitor leg extension at 135 and 165 degrees. Utilizing time lines on the goniogram, or by calculating elapsed time from paper speed, would considerably reduce human error. Also, an allowance of 3 to 5 degrees may be permitted and considered before declaring termination of the exercise.

Refinement can also take the form of wiring a simple a.c. circuit which allows for precise monitoring of duration of extension at each position.

Discussion Topics

1. Relate fatigue to rotatory force component, speed of performance, and power.

* From Dempster.[3]
† See page 89.

2. Is the term "explosive power" appropriate in describing muscle function? Define and document.

3. From a mechanical viewpoint, define and draw a more efficient human being than the one now inhabiting the earth.

4. How would you proceed to structure biomechanics into "physical fitness" norms? Enumerate. Define your terms.

Concluding Remarks

Force is a more precise term than strength. Being a vector quantity, force expresses magnitude as well as direction. Although force can be used in a variety of ways it remains explicit, e.g., one might speak of pulling force, exerted force, applied force, and gravitational force, moment of force, force arms—all appropriate to a discussion of man in a variety of physical expressions.

Laboratory Exercise 9 was conducted without the use of ergometric apparatus. Unsophisticated ergometers utilizing pulleys (which merely change direction of force) could have been suggested. They are non-essential to the purpose of demonstrating what was presented with minimal equipment. Many types of sophisticated apparatus are available —at great financial outlay. Transducers,* variously called strain gauges, add a new exact dimension to accuracy of multidimensional measurement: all force vectors can be monitored.

Precise assessment of cross-sectional area of human muscle can be achieved by means of ultrasonic photography. Ikai and Fukunaga[5] used such a technique which incorporates a circulating, ultrasonic scanner, a transducer, plethysmograph, and oscilloscope. Photographs of the cross-sectional view of the arm reveal a remarkably clear outline of the humerus, the location of fat deposits, and the presence of fascia.

While the focus of this publication is the laboratory exercise, departure into a relevant and related topic area appears justifiable. The researcher must rely on the subject's honor that "maximum force was exerted"; however, deception techniques can and must be structured into the research design to ensure the acquisition of valid, reliable data. In this area of muscle force, work, power, and endurance, man (and woman) is an "underachiever" who only occasionally exhibits super-normal feats, especially when personal glory is at stake or when life is endangered.†

Muscle force capability of the sexes is a question often raised. Apparently, muscle tissue is sexless. Measured differences in muscle force capability which favors the male usually reflect (1) cultural and environmental influences which affect women and are expressed through the psychological brake mechanism, (2) deficient experimental controls, and

* Mechanical-electrical devices which convert physical changes discernible as pressures, stresses, strains, and light levels into electrical variation which is observable on an oscilloscope, meter, or recorder.

† *The Guinness Book of Records*[6] (p. 340) provides interesting figures relative to weight lifting achievements. Most astonishing is the account of Mrs. Maxwell Rogers of Tampa, Florida, who, in 1960, reputedly lifted an end of a car weighing approximately 1635 kg (1.6 tons) which had pinned her son to the ground after the jack collapsed. Mrs. Rogers weighed 55.85 kg (123 lb. or 0.0615 ton!).

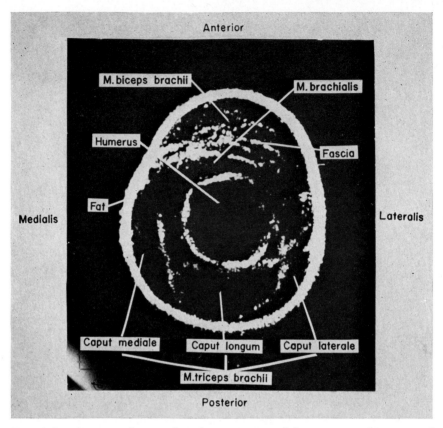

Fig. 4–5. Ultrasonic photography of cross-section of human arm. (Courtesy of Dr. Michio Ikai and Druck von J. P. Peter, Rothenburg.)

(3) the unrealistic technique of reporting force *per se* without relating it to essential, important, muscle cross-sectional areas or to mechanical considerations as reflected in moments of force. In a study involving 352 male and 359 female Philadelphians (between 8 and 22 years of age), Rodahl and associates[8] observed very little difference in the "strength" of the biceps muscle among members of the group, regardless of age or sex. Force was expressed per square centimeter of muscle cross-section. In a study involving a Japanese population of 119 males and 126 females, Ikai and Fukunaga[5] reported that "arm strength was fairly proportional to the cross-sectional area of the upper arm regardless of age and sex. . . . The strength per unit cross-sectional area (range: 4 kg/cm² to 8 kg/cm²) was almost the same in male and female regardless of age. In addition to that, there was not found any significant difference in ordinary and trained adult."

REFERENCES

1. Clark, G.: A method of computing the cross-section of the chest for children at seven, eight, and nine years. *Hum. Biol.* 2:539–546, 1930.

2. Dashiell, J. F.: Experimental studies of the influence of social situations on the behavior of individual human adults. *In* Murchison, C. A. (Ed.). *Handbook of Social Psychology,* Vol 2. New York, Russell and Russell, 1935.

3. Dempster, W. T.: Space requirements of the seated operator: geometrical, kinematic, and mechanical aspects of the body with special reference to the limbs. WADC Technical Report 55–159, Wright Air Development Center, Air Research and Development Command, U.S.A.F., Wright-Patterson AFB, Ohio, July 1955.

4. Dempster, W. T.: Free-body diagrams as an approach to the mechanics of human posture and locomotion. *In* Evans, F. G. (Ed.): *Biomechanical Studies of the Musculo-Skeletal System.* Springfield, Charles C Thomas, Publisher, 1961.

5. Ikai, M., and Fukunaga, T.: Calculation of muscle strength per unit cross-sectional area of human muscle by means of ultrasonic measurement. *Arbeitsphysiol.,* 26:26–32, 1968.

6. McWhirter, N., and McWhirter, R. (Eds.): *The Guinness Book of Records,* 14th Ed. London, Guinness Superlatives Ltd., 1967.

7. Morris, C. B.: The measurement of the strength of muscle relative to the cross-section. *Res. Quart.,* 19:295–303, 1948.

8. Rodahl, K., Astrand, P. O., Birkhead, N. C., Hettinger, T., Issekutz, B., Jr., Jones, D. M., and Weaver, R.: Physical work capacity. A study of some children and Young adults in the United States. *Arch. Environ. Health,* 2:499–510, 1961.

Chapter

5

REACTION TIME (RT) AND
MOVEMENT TIME (MT)

Preparation for this laboratory session requires the reading and comprehension of Chapter 2, *Muscle Considerations,* and, in particular, Chapter 3, *Neural Control of Muscle Activity,* of the text, *Physiological Basis of Human Performance* by B. Ricci (Philadelphia, Lea & Febiger, 1967).

Man is capable of fast action. After unwittingly touching a hot object, he jerks his finger away. This immediate reaction is made possible by nociceptive receptors and cortical level involvement. In such a situation, man does *not* engage in logic: "the pain is excruciating, therefore, I must remove my finger from the source of the pain." Later, if he wishes, he may recapitulate and evaluate the unpleasant experience.

The sudden decompression of an aircraft at high altitude (approximately 12,000 meters or 40, 000 feet) allows the pilot and crew the luxury of approximately *15 seconds* to adjust by switching to oxygen under pressure. Failure to react instantaneously may result in loss of consciousness and the attendant consequences. Fifteen seconds TUC* time represents the short interval during which the crew member must react to an unmistakable stimulus which he hears, feels, and sees. Because the emergency procedure has been rehearsed, the reaction is carried out quickly and efficiently. The crew member seemingly acts instinctively; he acts first and thinks† later.

The driver or passenger of an automobile that plunges into a shallow lake has at least a few seconds in which to decide on a course of action. He may act first, think later. Ideally, he should think first—and possibly

---

* TUC time, in air force parlance, means time of useful consciousness.
† A process involving mind, the organ of reasoning.

73

wait until the water pressure is equalized on both sides of the car door
—then act.

Although the gravity of situations differs, the biochemical and neuro-
muscular responses are similar in that all involve receptors, afferent and
efferent neural pathways, repolarization, and reflex action.

In the preceding presentations, reactions to varied stimuli and engage-
ment in variable courses of action were illustrated. Recognition of the
stimulus denotes the reaction phase; engaging in a definite course of
action constitutes the movement phase. Taken together, the phases may
be classified as total response time.

Discussion

At first thought it appears that reaction and movement times can be
easily and adequately monitored merely by depressing stopwatch stems.
Perusal of certain publications reinforces this idea; however, it is inescap-
able that the researcher, whose task it is to depress the stopwatch stem,
compounds the problem by *mixing in* his own reaction time. The question arises as to whose reaction time is being measured: that of the researcher or of the subject.

Not the least convincing is the reporting of reliability data of the stopwatch. A coefficient of correlation of 0.999—obtained from data resulting
from simultaneous depression of two stopwatch stems—might not reveal
the random error of measurement since watches A and B are being compared only to each other. Obviously, the use of a reliable standard must
be employed in order to compare watch A and then watch B to the
standard. Even assuming the use of the most precise chronometer, random error will be introduced by human triggering, i.e., depression of
watch stem with bars, levers, or fingers or other body parts. Human-trig-
gered stopwatches are acceptable for gross measurements only.

Electrically operated clocks plus momentary switches and microswitches are advocated in order to reduce source of error. More precise
timers, e.g., electronic counters, are available; however, emphasis in all
laboratory exercises in this publication is placed on relatively inexpensive
yet precise apparatus.

Laboratory Exercise Number 10—Measuring Reaction Time (RT) and Movement Time (MT)

Required Apparatus and Materials*
2 Precision timers
1 Lever switch, multiple circuit
1 Microswitch, push button or leaf
1 Double-pole single-throw switch
Copper conducting hook-up wire (at least 4 different colors of outer insulation preferred)
4 No. 15 dry cells (1.5 volt each)
1 Buzzer or bell, 6 volt
4 Minigators, insulated alligator clips
3 Jiffy box chassis† 4 inches in length, 2 inches wide, and 2¾ inches in depth

Definition of Terms

Reaction time is the interval of time that begins with the application of stimulus and ends with initial, ensuing action of muscle. Stimuli are of many types, but at least one or a combination of the following is involved: chemical, electrical, mechanical, or thermal. Higher brain centers may also be involved, as when response is elicited by a buzzer or bell or an illuminated lamp. Thus, stimuli may also be of the audio, visual, or tactile type. In the audio type, reaction time is the time interval between the initial sound and its identification by the subject. Also in evidence is the gross nature of the reaction time. In the stimulation of the muscle fiber bundle the reaction time is synonymous with the latent period, when repolarization takes place.‡ In the response to audio stimuli, reaction time embraces the time interval required for gross muscle action to occur and the latent period is included within the infinitely larger elapsed time interval. For the present experiments, the gross aspect of reaction time will be observed.

The assessment of reaction time requires an agreement between researcher and subject relative to mode of response. Reaction time may be simple or complex. Whatever the classification, a definite course of action must be agreed upon before data are collected.

* For approximate cost and for suggested timer source, see Appendix B, page 198.
† Switches can be mounted on panels or on wooden bases, depending largely upon the nature of the experiment.
‡ Some researchers have fractionated reaction time into reflex latency and motor components.

Movement time is an extension of the agreement between subject and researcher. After the completion of the reaction phase, the subject moves physically to a specified target. With targets close at hand, movement time may be equal to or less than reaction time. As target distances are increased, movement time will obviously exceed reaction time.

Procedure

The student is urged to exercise caution when working with alternating current sources. A sound rule to follow is that of connecting the electric timer to the 115V alternating-current source as the final step. Before probing or physically tracing the circuit, the source of the alternating current should be disconnected. It is also helpful to color code the circuit; this will help the student to visualize the completed circuit.

1. Wire the circuit depicted in Figure 5–1. The placement of switches 1, 2, and 3 is dependent upon the space requirements of the laboratory as well as the purpose of the experiment.

2. Secure SW2 on a lab bench directly before a chair in which subject will be seated.

3. Secure SW3 50 cm to the right of SW2.

4. Position buzzer or bell behind SW2.

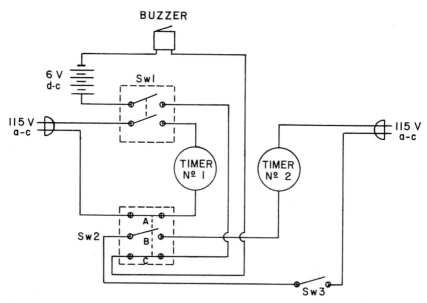

Fig. 5–1.   Schema of an alternating current-direct current circuit for the measurement of reaction time and movement time. Switch 1 (SW1) is (NO) normally open type. Switch 2 (SW2) is leaf type. When B is closed, A and C are opened. Switch 3 (SW3) is normally closed type (NC).

Switch 1 should be located in an adjacent room or behind a shield in order to reduce the subject's anticipatory movement.

Precautions must be taken to assure uniformity of alignment of subjects' arm and body positions (including position of feet).

Allow each subject a minimum of ten trials in order that he may become familiar with the feel of the switches, the placement of the switches, and the alignment of the body and arm in relation to SW2.

Following the familiarization routine, subjects may then proceed to establish control values. Order of testing must be agreed upon and adhered to. The matter of failing to stop the clock which monitors movement time because of misses generated by haste must be reconciled. Ten trials are suggested per bout and the best five reaction times and movement times are utilized in each bout. Four bouts per subject are advocated.

Data Treatment

1. Compute the group mean ($\overline{X}$) and standard deviation (s) for reaction time (RT) and movement time (MT) for each bout.

2. Plot the group results graphically; time in hundredths seconds (on ordinate) as a function of bouts (on abscissa). Depict $\overline{RT}$ with an open dot (○), $\overline{MT}$ with a closed dot (●), and express (s) as a vertical bar extending from ($\overline{X}$) of each measure.

Additional Notes

The reader may question the combination of direct-current and alternating-current circuits. This has been purposeful; it reinforces the basics of electricity learned in physics relative especially to direct-current cells which are additive in voltage (E). Note that the battery diagrammed in Figure 5–1 consists of four 1.5V cells in *series* arrangement; thus the total output is theoretically* 6V (1.5V × 4 = 6.0V) which supplies the requirements of the buzzer. It might also be noted that buzzer requirements are not critical at 6V but are generally within a range, e.g., 3V–6V.

Numerous circuit modifications are possible and the student is urged to experiment. For example, the battery source can be eliminated and replaced by a step-down transformer, thus making the circuit purely alternating current. The 6V source, tapped from the transformer, would supply the requirements of the buzzer or bell. Or, a 115V alternating-current buzzer or bell could be incorporated thereby eliminating the need

---

* Voltage decrease (a result of age or usage of cell) is ultimately related to depletion of chemical stores and slowing down of the chemical reaction within the cell.

for the step-down transformer; however, a relay would need to be incorporated. Timers operating only on direct current can be purchased, thus the circuit could become purely a direct-current one.

Circuits can be purely alternating current or purely direct current or a combination alternating current-direct current as depicted in Figure 5–1. Note that alternating current-direct current circuits are adjacent but *separate*. Burned-out meters and electrical fires can result from the operation of direct-current meters with an alternating-current source and vice versa. When in doubt, review the basics of electricity or converse with the instructor.

Discussion Topics

1. Define and present an example of discriminative (complex) reaction time.

2. How are reaction time and movement time related to recruitment and to gradation of contraction?

3. What effect does eye or limb preference have on reaction and movement times?

4. How does latent period relate to reaction time?

Laboratory Exercise Number 11—Effect of Heat and of Cold on Reaction Time and Movement Time of Preferred Limb

Required Apparatus

The same apparatus is used as that required for Laboratory Exercise Number 10.

Definition of Terms

Read "Definition of Terms" on pages 75–76.

As used here, *preferred limb* refers to the limb which is controlled with greater ease.

Procedure

In general the procedure is similar to that required for Laboratory Exercise Number 10 except that the split-half treatment method will be used, i.e., one half of the group will start with the cold treatment, the other half with the heat treatment. Upon completion of ten trials within each sequence by all members of the group the treatments will be reversed.

The order of testing within each treatment must be adhered to.

Application of heat and of cold may take many forms. Perhaps the most accessible form is that of limb immersion. A plastic tub of sufficient size to accommodate the forearm is necessary.

Chipped ice, occasionally added, will serve to maintain the desired water temperature (10° C). Care must be taken to agitate the water periodically. Immersion should be of 10 minutes' duration.

Immersion of the forearm in hot water (38° C) should also be of 10 minutes' duration.

Unless extra class time is utilized, only a manageable number of subjects will be required to participate (see *Additional Notes*).

Data Treatment

1. Compute the group mean ($\overline{X}$), standard deviation (s), and standard error of the mean ($S\overline{X}$) for RT and MT for each treatment.

2. Plot the individual results graphically. Depict RT with an open circle (○) and $\overline{MT}$ with an open triangle (▽) for cold treatment and $\overline{RT}$ (•), $\overline{MT}$ (▼) for hot treatment.

NOTE: A study of the effects of heat and cold on reaction and movement times is ideally suited to analysis of variance, two-way classification computation. Because a study of this type involves one group of subjects with repeated measures, three variance components will be identified: between treatments, i.e., heat application and cold application, between subjects, and, finally, treatments-by-subjects interaction. The F ratio is obtained by dividing the mean squares of treatments by the mean squares for the treatments-by-subjects interaction.

Additional Notes

Cold or heat application might take many forms. Immersion of the forearm in water is easily accomplished. The use of whirlpool baths, when available, is suggested for heat application.

Various forms of dry heat (provided by bakers or short infrared lamps) or of moist heat (hot towels or hydrocolator pads) may also be used.

In such a laboratory exercise as this, contrasting skin surface temperatures are assured. The extent of the shell temperature changes can be ascertained through skin thermocouples (see p. 107). The extent of limb muscle temperature changes or the extent of vasodilatation or of vasoconstriction in the limb can be monitored, but this is beyond the scope of this laboratory exercise.

Sound organizational procedures require the overlapping of cold application (and later of heat application) in order that the apparatus be effectively utilized within the prescribed laboratory period. During any time interval, two subjects must be receiving the pre-test treatment:

Subject	Elapsed Time of Treatment (min)	Elapsed Time of Testing Interval (min)
A	0–10	10–15
B	5–15	15–20
C	10–20	20–25
D	15–25	25–30
n		

By following this format, four subjects can be tested during each half-hour interval.

Discussion Topics

1. What are the probable reasons for differences in reaction time caused by cold and heat?

2. What application to physical or athletic performance can you make of the results gained from this laboratory exercise?

3. What probable effect will low discomfort tolerance levels to cold (or to heat) have on reaction time and movement time?

4. What probable movement time differences will be observable among individuals of varying forearm densities?

Laboratory Exercise Number 12—Effect of Normal Versus Reduced Blood Flow in Upper Limb on Reaction Time and Movement Time

Required Apparatus

The same apparatus is required as for Laboratory Exercise Number 10 with:

*Additional Apparatus**

Sphygmomanometer, mercurial type

Definition of Terms

Reread "Definition of Terms" section for Laboratory Exercise Number 10.

Procedure

The procedure is similar to that followed in Laboratory Exercise Number 10. The order of testing must be adhered to.

1. Prior to this laboratory exercise, the systolic blood pressure of each individual must be estimated. (See pp. 39–40 for procedural steps in estimating systolic blood pressure.) Record these pressures for each individual.

2. Wire circuit as in Figure 5–1.

3. Subject undergoes reaction time and movement time testing. *Five trials are taken.* (The best three reaction times and movement times will be utilized in each bout.)

4. Maintain consecutive order of testing.

5. Wrap the sphygmomanometer cuff around the arm (above the elbow) of the first subject and inflate to a pressure which is 20 mm Hg less than the subject's systolic blood pressure (estimated earlier; see step 1 above).

6. Following a *one-minute* interval of pressure application, the subject undergoes reaction time and movement time testing. Note that *during* the testing period, the cuff pressure is maintained.

7. To reduce the subject's discomfort, record *five* trials. (The best three reaction times and movement times will be utilized in each bout.)

* For approximate cost, see Appendix B, page 198.

Data Treatment

1. Compute the group mean ($\overline{X}$), standard deviation (s), standard error of the mean ($\overline{SX}$) for RT and $\overline{MT}$ for each treatment.

2. Plot the individual results graphically. RT (○), MT (▽) normal blood flow; $\overline{RT}$ (●), $\overline{MT}$ (▼) reduced blood flow.

NOTE: Effects of normal and reduced forearm blood flow on reaction and movement time is also ideally suited to analysis of variance, two-way classification computation. Because a laboratory exercise of this type involves one group of subjects with repeated measures, three variance components will be identified: between treatments, i.e., normal blood flow and restricted blood flow, between subjects, and, finally, treatments-by-subjects interaction. The F ratio is obtained by dividing the mean squares of treatments by the mean squares for the treatments-by-subjects interaction.

Additional Notes

Quick release coupling and an Extendex* cord is advocated. The quick release coupling will permit the use of a single manometer. Several inflatable cuffs can be pressed into service thereby reducing the length of the between-subject delays. The Extendex cord affords greater freedom for the subject. Obviously, several separate sphygmomanometers could be used.

Each subject is urged to put forth his best effort; however, in a laboratory exercise such as this, varying levels of discomfort tolerance may introduce wide variation.

Discussion Topics

1. Discuss, in physiological terms, the results of the laboratory exercise.
2. Discuss, biochemically, the effect of prolonged, restricted blood flow to any limb.
3. Relate restricted blood flow during isometric exercise routines to endurance.
4. Explain, neuromuscularly, the "heavy-limb" feeling associated with the occluding pressure of the inflated cuff.

---

* Extendex is a registered trade mark of the W. A. Baum Co. Inc., of Copiague, New York 11726.

Concluding Remarks

The versatility of the basic circuit (see Fig. 5–1) is pronounced. With minor modifications, many additional laboratory sessions can be generated. For example, SW3 can be placed 50 meters from SW2 thus enabling the student to measure the reaction time and movement time involved in the 50-meter dash, low or high hurdles, or obstacle course running. Other possible uses include the measurement of reaction time (to a coach's signal or cue) and movement time between first and second base or between any bases. Circuit modifications would include the use of mat switches* or embedded microswitches to replace the leaf switches and microswitches depicted in Figure 5–1.

The attempt in this chapter has been to suggest how reaction time and movement time can be measured accurately with small financial outlay.

With additional clocks and leaf switches, the speed of running, as well as the acceleration and velocity, can be measured *during* particular segments of the 50-meter dash.

More sophistication can be introduced—at added cost. For example, the MARK-Q-MATIC,† coupled with a tape recorder, lends itself to studies of reaction and movement times of football linemen, ends, or backs, to the quarterback's inflection, or rhythmical or nonrhythmical cadences (Fig. 5–2).

Additional financial outlay can ensure greater precision of measurement. For example, electronic timers capable of recording to 0.001 second (with precision of 0.1 percent) can replace the 0.01-second timers. Electronic beams can also be used. Time delay, stimulus-controlled reaction timers are commercially available at prices ranging from $250 to $700.

An example of the sophisticated apparatus deemed essential to research involving reaction time, reflex time, reflex latency, and nerve conduction velocity is demonstrated in the article by Kroll.[4] Reaction time in advanced research is fractionated into pre-motor (reflex latency) and motor components.

The order of testing suggested in these laboratory exercises is based upon expediency and is quite different from the testing order which would be followed in an experimental situation. For example, in an attempt to rule out possible sequence of measurements effects, i.e., practice and

---

* Or ribbon, step, and foot switches. Available from Tapeswitch Corp. Source: Allied Electronics, 100 N. Western Ave., Chicago, Illinois 60680.

† MARK-Q-MATIC is a registered trademark of General Techniques Inc., 1270 Broadway, New York, N. Y. 10001.

learning effect, the order of testing per subject might follow a sequence as:

1	2	3
2	3	1
3	1	2
2	1	3
3	2	1
1	3	2

(Conditions: 1 control; 2 cold; 3 heat)

Structured into the experimental design would be sufficient allotments of time between conditions.

For the reader who wishes to peruse additional sources related to reaction time, the following publications are suggested. A dictionary of psy-

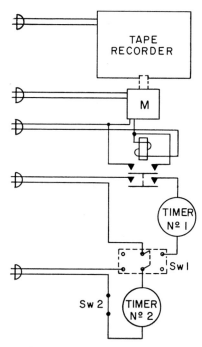

Fig. 5–2.   Arrangement for reaction and movement time studies of subjects to voice commands. The location on the tape of the specific voice command is marked. (Ease of location is enhanced by playback of tape at slow speed.) With the MARK-Q-MATIC located to the *right* of the recorder (adjacent to take-up reel) a 13-mm mark is made with a machine scoring or No. 2 pencil, on the tape center preceding the specific voice command at a location determined by the distance between the playback head and MARK-Q-MATIC poles. In actuality, this is not a voice-triggered circuit. The MARK-Q-MATIC—essentially a combination sensing device and relay—is activated by the pencil mark on the tape which completes the electrical circuit across its poles and triggers the clock. Other relay depicted is DPST 115V a.c., holding type.

chological and psychoanalytical terms has been prepared by English and English.[3] Teichner[6] has reviewed simple reaction time studies. In the opinion of Teichner, ". . . the following generalizations appear to have been reasonably well established."

"1. There is a positive correlation between the visual and the auditory RT.

"2. Simultaneous stimulation of more than one sense modality produces faster RT's than stimulation of just one. On the other hand, successive stimulation of different senses produces slower RT's than stimulation of a single sensory channel.

"3. For visual and thermal RT's the greater the extent of the stimulus in space, i.e. the greater the number of receptors stimulated, the faster the speed of reaction up to some limit.

"4. Under daylight or illuminated conditions the visual RT becomes longer the greater the distance of stimulation from the fovea.

"5. In the case of each receptor system, RT is a negatively accelerated decreasing function of intensity up to some maximum intensity value after which RT either becomes suddenly lengthened, the function at this point being discontinuous, or asymptotic to a physiological limit.

"6. RT is a slowly falling growth function of chronological age until about 30 years after which it is a slowly rising function.

"7. In general the RT of the human male is faster than that of the female.

"8. The optimum foreperiod of RT may be thought of as lying in a range between approximately 1.5 and 8.0 sec. Its position in this range is determined by a large number of factors including the duration and intensity of the warning signal and of the stimulus, and the amount, locus, and time of production of muscular tension.

"9. RT is not related to the length, direction, or speed of movement of the responding member.

"10. Under vigilance conditions, the longer the period during which S must respond, the longer the RT."

In the practical statistical sense, bivariate data ordinarily exhibit a relationship which increases as the specificity of each measure is increased. Not only is the correlation between the measures increased, the predictive power is also increased. The reader whose interests embrace the research aspect of reaction and response time might ponder the wisdom and accept the admonishment of a Frenchman and an Englishman.

Addressing himself to the topic of general reaction time, Pacaud[5] noted:

"Under these conditions it appears to us ill founded to speak of a general reaction time in a subject without specifying the nature of the movement to which it is linked.

"It follows that the reaction time of a single group of movements is far from being sufficient as indicating a general characteristic of an individual.".

Bartlett[1] suggests that:

". . . the beginnings of skill are to be found in the graded response. [That] most of our everyday actions seem to be more or less graded in amount, direction, duration, and other respects in agreement with corresponding variations in the stimuli required to produce them. And such graded action, however simple it may be, has at least one of the fundamental marks of skill—an effector response is not merely set off by a receptor function but is guided and determined by it. . . . Skill, then, whether bodily or mental has from the beginning this character of being in touch with demands which come from the outside world."

Pointing out the significant results of experimental studies of skill, Bartlett[1] concludes:

"By far the most important [result] is that no measure of isolated function can throw any light upon skill or immediate skill potentiality."

Bartlett[2] also suggests:

"The best single measure of skill level is one of its 'range of constancy,' its degree of resistance to disintegrating conditions. . . . If level of skill is defined by its capacity to resist interference, the measuring of total timing of successive responses is the best single criterion, for if timing gets out of step nothing can for long stop the complete break up of the skill."

Only through exhaustive, precise, and controlled experimentation can questions relating to optimum use of man's physical talents be resolved.

REFERENCES

1. Bartlett, F. C.: The measurement of human skill. The nature of skill. *Brit. Med. J., 1*:835–838, 1947.

2. Bartlett, F. C.: The measurement of human skill. The grouping and stability of the constituent items in skill performance. *Brit. Med. J., 1*:877–880, 1947.

3. English, H. B., and English, A. C.: *A Comprehensive Dictionary of Psychological and Psychoanalytical Terms.* New York, Longmans, Green and Co., 1958.

4. Kroll, W.: Patellar reflex time and reflex latency under Jendrassik and crossed extensor facilitation. *Amer. J. Phys. Med., 47*:292–301, 1968.

5. Pacaud, S.: Contribution à l'étude des mouvements volontaires. *L'Année Psycholgique, 40*:152–170, 1939.

6. Teichner, W. H.: Recent studies of simple reaction time. *Psych. Bull., 51*:128–149, 1954.

Chapter

6

ASSESSING JOINT RANGE OF MOVEMENT

Chapter 4, especially pages 54–58 and 70–73, in the text, *Physiological Basis of Human Performance,* by B. Ricci (Philadelphia, Lea & Febiger, 1967) constitutes recommended reading. A review of direct current electricity is also recommended.

One function of the human frame, or skeleton, is that of affording protection to the vital organs; however, a number of organs are relatively unprotected (viz., kidneys, stomach, intestines, and external reproductive organs). Another function of the skeleton is that of providing an extensive series of levers which are acted upon by muscle tissue. This enables man to move and to express himself physically. Man is designed for motion.

Discussion

Motion is generally described qualitatively and, often, colorfully. Accomplished gymnasts perform *gracefully*. A balletomane may be moved to describe a dance as *fluid motion*. Sport scribes continue to coin new words and phrases which qualitatively describe athletic performance.

Quantitative assessment of physical performance can be achieved through the application of cinematography. This is neither an inexpensive venture nor one without attendant problems such as parallax errors and the synchronization of cameras in multiplane analysis of motion. The time lag resulting from film processing is also present.

Laboratory exposure to the assessment of joint range of motion is beneficial if the technique yields valid and reliable data. Until the invention of the elgon* by Karpovich[9] reliable quantification of joint range of movement by inexpensive means was unattainable.

At the present time, elgon range of movement assessment is limited to

---

* Elgon is a contraction of electric goniometer.

hinge joints (diarthroses ginglymus) and pivotal joints (diarthroses tro-
choid). Assessment of joint range of movement in a single plane constitutes another limitation.

In the ensuing discussion, the words *motion* (change of position) and
movement (manner of motion) will be used interchangeably.

From the circuit diagram depicted in Figure 6–1 the reader's attention is directed to the 9V direct-current source provided by the two batteries. Note the relative position of each battery. This circuit is described
as a "bucking circuit," i.e., the current flow in one leg of the circuit
"bucks" the current flow in the opposite circuit. This is not to be confused with a Wheatstone bridge circuit which could replace the present
arrangement; however, the substitution of the Wheatstone bridge circuit
would increase the cost rather than contribute to the precision of the
elgon.

The Wheatstone or simple bridge circuit consists of a network of four
resistors,* two of which are usually fixed types with the remaining
resistors being variable types. The galvanometer, the bridge across the
parallel branches of the circuit, will indicate zero current flow when the
circuit is balanced, i.e., equal resistance in each leg of the circuit.

---

* The reader will recall that the basic requirements of a Wheatstone bridge circuit
include an emf source and galvanometer in addition to the resistors.

Laboratory Exercise Number 13—Estimation of Range of Movement of Left Knee and Ankle during Bench Stepping

*Required Apparatus and Materials**

Two-channel control circuit† includes elgons, protractor, and chassis (base to which components are attached)

Two elgon chasses including brass hinges (½ inch × ⁷⁄₁₆ inch wide open), snap fasteners

Recorder, two channel minimum

Adhesive tape, 1-inch wide

Skin-marking pencil

Wooden bench

Definition of Terms

By convention, quantification of range of movement is based upon words or terms which describe both *position* and *direction.* Also by convention, three basic planes of motion are described in relation to the anatomical position.‡ These planes, which are imaginary, appear at first to be unwieldy. However, the reader will conquer confusion if he will consider *erect* to mean straight; *vertical* should be considered in an anatomical rather than physical sense. Vertical refers to the vertex or crown of the head; thus, one can visualize a plane extending from head to foot. With these adoptions, the following definitions apply irrespective of body position.

1. *Median* plane. An anteroposterior or vertical plane dividing the body into right (dextral) and left (sinistral) halves. *Sagittal* is often used interchangeably with *median;* however, *sagittal* is more correctly employed to describe a plane *parallel* to the *median* plane.

2. *Frontal* or *coronal* plane. A lateral, vertical plane which intersects the median plane at a right angle thus dividing the body into anterior and posterior parts.

3. *Horizontal* plane. This plane, at a right angle to *both* median and

---

* For approximate cost, see Appendix B, page 199.

† NOTE: A single channel is depicted in Figure 6–1. Additional channels would NOT require additional microammeters or batteries but would require the remaining parts depicted. These would be wired in parallel circuitry with the battery source and microammeter.

‡ The anatomical position is an erect position in which the upper limbs are extended alongside the lateral aspect of the trunk and thighs. The forearms are rotated laterally thus exposing the palms; the toes are directed forward.

frontal planes, separates the upper from the lower portion of the body. *Transverse* is used interchangeably with horizontal.

Direction of movement, except for abduction and adduction, is more easily comprehended without reference to the planes.* The following definitions reflect this:

1. *Flexion* is exemplified by a *reduction* in joint angle.

2. *Extension* is exemplified by an *increase* in joint angle.

3. *Abduction,* occurring in the *coronal* plane, denotes movement of a body part or limb *away* from the midline.

4. *Adduction,* antonymous to abduction, signifies movement of a body part or limb *toward* the midline in the *coronal* plane.

5. *Supination* describes an exposure of the *anterior* surface of the body. Thus, lateral rotation of the forearm results in exposure of the anterior aspect of the hand—the palm.

6. *Pronation,* antonym of supination, signifies an exposure of the *posterior* surface of the body. Medial rotation of the forearm exposes the *dorsum* of the hand.

7. *Inversion* is descriptive of movements of the foot in which exposure of the *plantar* surface, directed *medially,* is attempted.

8. *Eversion,* the antonym of inversion, indicates foot movement during which the attempted exposure of the *plantar* surface is directed *laterally.*

9. *Rotation* is a form of movement about a *longitudinal* axis. Medial and lateral applied to rotation describe nonspecific forms of rotation (see 5, 6, 7, 8 above).

10. *Circumduction* is descriptive of movement which sequentially involves flexion—extension interspersed with abduction—adduction. Articulation centers at the proximal portion of the joint while the distal portion of the segment may describe a complete excursion (360 degrees).

Obviously, movement of this type can occur only within joints classified as diarthroses condyloid or diarthroses enarthrosis (see text p. 55).

Ohm's law provides an explanation of the interrelationship between electromotive force, resistance, and current in a direct-current electric circuit. The intensity of an electric current passing through a conductor is *directly* proportional to the electromotive force and *inversely* proportional to the resistance afforded by the conductor: $E = IR$, $I = E/R$. Ohm's law applies to a complete circuit or to any part of the circuit.

The *elgon* consists of a *potentiometer* within an adujstable circular housing which includes snap-button studs. Sockets for the studs are located on the *chassis* (see text p. 70).

Goniogram refers to the oscillographic or pen recording of the elgon.

* The author is cognizant of the definition which appears in a number of anatomy texts: "Flexion and extension occur in the sagittal plane." This is too rigid! Are not the arms *flexed* in a person with arms akimbo? Is not this the coronal plane?

Procedure

   Assembling components and wiring the control panel, elgon, and control panel to the recorder will require the services of an electronics technician for several hours. This task also qualifies as a special project for a class.

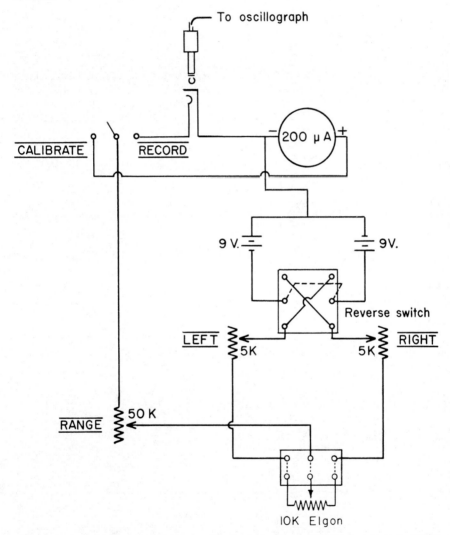

Fig. 6–1.   Schematic of one elgon control circuit. Record-calibrate switch is SPDT (single pole double throw) toggle type. Left and right positioning controls are necessary during circuit balancing phase. Range control is used to adjust sensitivity. The elgon is depicted at the bottom of the schema. The reverse switch is not necessary; it constitutes a convenience item. Additional channels can be added as needed; however, only one microammeter can serve all channels.

The following assumptions are held: (1) the circuit has been wired as shown in Figure 6–1, (2) the wiper contact plus both terminals of the circular potentiometer* is joined to the three-prong plug† by a two-meter length of wire and, (3) the control panel is wired to the recorder.

1. Turn recorder ON. NOTE: Oscillographs require a specified "warm-up" period. Generally, one-half hour is considered sufficient; consult the recorder manual for precise time interval.

2. Snap-fasten the elgon to the calibration protractor. NOTE: In the following example, the elgon will be balanced at the 180-degree position; therefore, manipulate moveable end until pointer is set at 90 degrees. Elgon is now in line. Adoption of the following arbitrary rule is suggested: Consider the elgon arm attached to the protractor indicator to correspond with the more moveable end of the chassis; therefore, in this situation (i.e. calibrating the elgon for the left knee) this arm will be fastened to the lower socket of the elgon chassis. NOTE: "Upper" and "lower" refer to the anatomical position.

3. Connect elgon plug to control panel input (see Fig. 6–2).

4. Turn LEFT positioning control to extreme left and RIGHT control to extreme right. Turn RANGE control to maximum sensitivity (minimum resistance).

5. Flip record-calibrate switch to CALIBRATE.

6. Turn LEFT and RIGHT positioning controls until microammeter needle centers and registers zero. In all likelihood one positioning control will require a greater amount of turning than the other will.

7. Indication of a balanced circuit is provided by observing the microammeter needle which must remain unaffected by:
   A. Any changes in RANGE control (turn to minimum sensitivity).
   B. The record-calibrate switch (flip from record to calibrate: repeat several times).
   NOTE: If difficulty is experienced in balancing the circuit, read step 17.

8. Connect phone jack from control panel to recorder; turn recorder to OPERATE (set paper speed at SLOW).

9. Flip record-calibrate switch to RECORD and obtain a calibration tracing by:
   A. Manipulating the galvanometer or the galvanometer position control (on oscillograph) or the pen marker control until the tracing for the 180-degree setting of the elgon is located at a convenient position on the recording paper which may be represented by a centrally located major grid line.

---

* B16–115 10K ohm potentiometer.
† Cinch-Jones type.

Fig. 6–2.   Control panel showing elgon on calibration protractor. Note micro-ammeter at left and channel 2 toggle switch in calibrate position.

B. Physically move the calibration protractor indicator 10 degrees to the right and note that the recorder has responded. At this juncture, RANGE sensitivity adjustments must be made in the interest of *standardization* and *convenience.*

   (1) *Standardization:* Karpovich has suggested the adoption of the following rule:

a. FLEXION, PRONATION, and ABDUCTION are recorded as *downward* tracings. When using an oscillograph recorder the above movements would correspond to a galvanometer trace deflection to the RIGHT.

b. EXTENSION, SUPINATION, and ADDUCTION are recorded as *upward* tracings. This would correspond to a galvanometer trace deflection to the LEFT.

(2) *Convenience.* Ease of determining the range of movement is based upon the ratio of the assigned pen deflection or trace light deflection to elgon movement. For example, 10 degree elgon movement corresponds conveniently with 1-cm deflection on the recorder.* Before establishing the ratio, one must consider:

a. The probable range of movement in the joint to be monitored.

b. The width of the recorder paper. This factor is basic.

c. If the recorder responds in the standardized manner [see 9B(1) above] then all that remains to be done is to determine the ratio of elgon movement to recorder deflection. Manipulation of the recorder deflection is accomplished by turning the RANGE control.

d. If the recorder does NOT respond in the accepted manner, the student has three choices available to him:

   i. Flip the REVERSE switch. This electrically reverses the elgon thereby changing the direction of recorder deflection. NOTE: When the reverse switch is used, *the circuit must again be balanced.*

   ii. Physically reverse the position of the elgon on the calibration protractor. On control panels that lack a reverse switch† this constitutes the only alternative.

   iii. Monitor the movement of a contralateral joint; however, this may prove to be inconvenient. For example, if an elgon has been calibrated for use on the left knee it can be used on the right knee *provided* it is placed on the chassis 180 degrees out of phase relative to its position on the calibration protractor.

10. After establishing the recorder deflection-elgon movement ratio,

---

* A worn or unclean potentiometer can cause deflections which differ from the ratio initially intended. In such cases, calculate a new ratio, e.g., from 180 to 110 degrees, 10 degrees = 1 cm ∴ 1 degree = 1 mm, but from 110 to 100 degrees, 10 degrees = 1.2 cm ∴ 1 degree = 1.2 mm. A deflection of 7.6 cm = 75 degrees. An alternative is to clean or to replace the worn potentiometer.

† See caption to Figure 6–1.

record a calibration tracing for the expected range of movement at the knee joint.

11. Place a flesh pencil mark on the subject's left leg (lateral aspects) at the following sites: midline of greater trochanter, center of joint rotation at the knee, and at the midline of the lateral malleolus.

12. Measure and record (in cm) the length of the left leg.

13. Tape the chassis on the lateral aspect of the subject's left leg. Align the chassis center over the center of joint rotation. The upper chassis arm should be aligned with the center of the greater trochanter, the lower chassis with the center of the lateral malleolus.

14. Remove elgon from calibration protractor and place on subject's left knee. NOTE: Upper arm of elgon must be snapped into upper chassis socket.

15. Fasten the wire to the shorts or other convenient location on clothing. Tape may be used or cloth may be gathered around the wire and fastened with a pin.

16. Instruct subject to flex the leg several times. Observe galvanometer trace deflection. NOTE: Conserve recorder paper by turning the paper control to OFF when it is not being used.

17. Assuming the control panel to be operative, i.e., switches and control potentiometers in working order, wiring intact, and batteries sound, the inability to balance the circuit may be due to the physical change of position of the elgon potentiometer. To rectify this condition:

A. Remove the circular potentiometer from its adjustable housing.

B. Estimate the approximate center of the carbon horseshoe by determining the full range of potentiometer movement then backing off one half the distance. NOTE: The use of an ohmmeter would aid in determining the exact electrical center. Rotate the potentiometer to determine maximum resistance, then rotate the potentiometer in the opposite direction until one half the maximum resistance is attained.

C. Set the housing arms at 180 degrees, and *being certain not to rotate the potentiometer,* secure it to the housing.

18. Following the same procedure, balance another elgon then calibrate it and attach it to the left ankle. Reference points for chassis attachment include: center of fibula head, center of lateral malleolus, and head of fifth metatarsal. NOTE: Of necessity, the lower arm of the elgon chassis will require cutting. (See Fig. 6–3.)

19. After both elgons are in place, instruct subject to perform a five-minute step test on the 40.6-cm bench. (Cadence: 25 steps/min; set metronome at 100.)

20. Jot down the recorder paper speed.

21. Obtain goniograms from each class member.

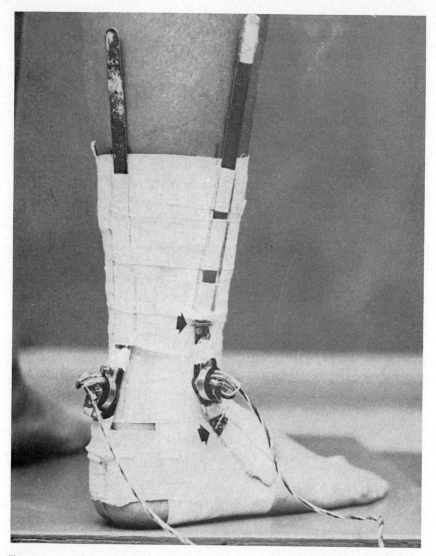

Fig. 6–3.   Elgons shown in position during measurement of sub-talar joint stability afforded by adhesive support. Elgon along Achilles tendon monitored inversion-eversion. (Note one arm of chassis bent under the heel.) Laterally placed elgon (pictured at right) monitored flexion-extension. Removable hinge pins (designated by arrows) afford the opportunity to remove elgons without disturbing alignment and permit the subject ease of movement during exercise phase.

Data Treatment

1. Measure the range of movement at each joint at the beginning of bench stepping and at the end of each minute of performance.

2. Draw stick figures on the goniogram depicting: (a) standing, (b) left foot being placed atop bench, (c) torque phase, (d) full standing atop bench, (e) return of left foot to floor, (f) standing.

3. Using class data, calculate coefficient of correlation of maximum knee flexion, at third minute, and length of limb.

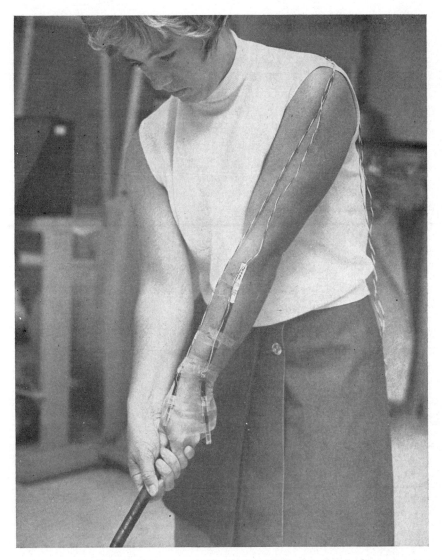

Fig. 6–4. Use of the miniature potentiometer. Note the chassis-sleeve arrangement. Flexion-extension wrist movements were monitored by medial elgon and abduction-adduction by elgon on dorsum of hand. (See Arnold.[1])

Additional Notes

Selection of a suitable speed for the recorder paper is related to the intended use of the goniogram. Fast paper speeds will spread out the goniogram, thus enabling more precise analysis of movement phases.

When light-sensitive paper is used (as with the oscillograph), certain precautions must be observed. Since the paper will develop when exposed to light, solid objects such as pencils or rulers placed on the paper during the self-development stage may obscure parts of the goniogram. For similar reasons, storage of the goniogram is safely and easily accomplished by rolling it up. Photographs of goniograms may be taken provided a yellow filter is used. For additional specific information the reader is referred to instructional folders provided by the manufacturer.

Waterproof elgons are described by Gollnick and Karpovich.[7]

Miniature elgons, also introduced by Karpovich, have been used.

Removable hinge pins in the metal chassis permit the removal of the elgon, allowing unrestricted movement during exercise (see Fig. 6–3). This technique may be used, for example, in research to determine the effectiveness of adhesive support to the ankle.

The recorder used in the University of Massachusetts Laboratory of Applied Physiology is an oscillograph (Honeywell 1508). Four of the channels, equipped with M 350 A galvanometers, serve a dual purpose. Through a switch circuit, four elgons can be monitored simultaneously. Or, these same channels can also monitor and record the inputs from a cardiotachometer, Beckman LB1 carbon dioxide analyzer, Beckman F3 oxygen analyzer, and an ECG unit.

Another local feature is that of directing the output from the control panel through a variable potentiometer (15K ohms) for each of the four recorder channels. This serves as a vernier for the magnitude of the spot deflection.

Discussion Topics

1. Observe a goniogram of five-minute step-testing. Can you present evidence of local muscular fatigue?

2. How would you handle a loss of linearity in the elgon (evidenced by the calibration curve)? Assume that elgons cannot be cleaned or replaced.

3. Discuss the goniogram in terms of Ohm's law.

4. Biomechanically considered, what conclusions can you draw from your data?

Concluding Remarks

The physical limitation provided by the wire which tethers the subject to the control panel and recorder is evident. As is reflected in the cited research articles, the logistics of the wire has not been a deterrent. Goniograms of knee and elbow movement of swimmers using the breast stroke, dolphin-butterfly, and crawl strokes have been obtained by Gollnick and Karpovich.[7] Certain gymnastic routines have been traced. Analysis of normal and pathological gait have been made by Finley and Karpovich[6] and by Tipton and Karpovich.[17] The walking gait, canter, and gallop of a Morgan horse owned by the University of Massachusetts has also been obtained.

Electrogoniometry has many additional applications. With its use, restoration of limb function following surgery or injury can be quantified. Goniograms of Harvard step-testing can confirm full knee and hip extension as well as the maintenance of proper cadence* (see Ricci et al.[16]). Event markers coupled with the elgon present an added dimension. By the use of a simple switch the release of objects such as footballs or baseballs can be indicated on the goniogram. (Actually the switch is a series circuit; a conductor attached to the object completes the circuit.) When the object leaves the fingers, for example, the circuit is broken and is so indicated on the recorder (see Arnold[1] as well as Gollnick and Karpovich[7]).

The elgon is routinely used with electromyography in laboratory exercises.

Karpovich and Ikai[8] have used the elgon in testing patellar reflex time and velocity of reflex movement. Doss and Karpovich[4] utilized the elgon in their assessment of muscular force at the elbow joint.

Varying degrees of success have been reported with telemetered elgons. Karpovich appears to have achieved success in his quest for an elgon capable of monitoring the excursions of a freely moveable joint. The device is currently being laboratory tested.

Modifications to the elgon have been introduced at the Moss Rehabilitation Hospital, Philadelphia, by Finley.[5]

The science of movement has been theoretically elucidated. The quantification of movement patterns has been reflected on goniograms and on film and has been computerized.

Displacement, horizontal and vertical components of force, moments of force, link systems, and body segment angular velocities and accelerations are examples of the terminology of the student of cinematography. Dempster[2,3] has achieved distinction. The contribution of Plagenhoef,[12-14]

---

* A time marker was used. The marker is a convenience item. Time intervals derived from the speed of recorder paper can be physically entered.

who has modified Dempster's technique, is commendable. Using the technique of Plagenhoef, Ricci[15] has analyzed the chinning-the-bar exercise. The technique of Nelson[11] is also praiseworthy (see also Larson and Nelson[10]).

Man is designed for motion; the design of man is to quantify motion.

REFERENCES

1. Arnold, G. B.: An electrogoniometric study of the degree of movement of the wrist joint during the golf swing. Unpublished Master's thesis, University of Massachusetts, 1968.

2. Dempster, W. T.: The anthropometry of body action. *Ann. N. Y. Acad. Sci., 63*:559–585, 1955a.

3. Dempster, W. T.: Free-body diagrams as an approach to the mechanics of posture and motion. *In* Evans, F. G. (Ed.): *Biomechanical Studies of the Musculo-Skeletal System.* Springfield, Ill., Charles C Thomas, Publisher, 1961.

4. Doss, W., and Karpovich, P. V.: A comparison of concentric, eccentric, and isometric strength of elbow flexors. *J. Appl. Physiol., 20*:351–353, 1965.

5. Finley, F. R., Cody, K., and Finizie, R.: Locomotion patterns in elderly women. *J. Phys. Med. & Rehab., 50*:140–146, 1969.

6. Finley, F. R., and Karpovich, P. V.: Electrogoniometric analysis of normal and pathological gaits. *Res. Quart., 35*:379–384, 1964.

7. Gollnick, P. D., and Karpovich, P. V.: Electrogoniometric study of locomotion and of some athletic movements. *Res. Quart., 35*:357–369, 1964.

8. Karpovich, P. V., and Ikai, M.: Relation between reflex and reaction time. *Fed. Proc., 19*:300, 1960.

9. Karpovich, P. V., and Karpovich, G. P.: Electrogoniometer. A new device for study of joints in action. *Fed. Proc., 18*:79, 1959.

10. Larson, C., and Nelson, R. C.: An analysis of strength, speed, and acceleration of elbow flexion. *J. Phys. Med. & Rehab., 50*:274–278, 1969.

11. Nelson, R. C., Petak, K. L., and Pechar, G. S.: Use of stroboscopic-photographic techniques in biomechanics research. *Res. Quart., 40*:424–426, 1969.

12. Plagenhoef, S. C.: Methods for obtaining kinetic data to analyze human motions. *Res. Quart., 37*:103–112, 1966.

13. Plagenhoef, S. C.: Joint moments of force in selected sports and rehabilitation exercises. *J. Phys. Mental Rehab., 21*:90–96, 1967.

14. Plagenhoef, S. C.: Computer programs for obtaining kinetic data on human movement. *J. Biomech., 1*:221–234, 1968.

15. Ricci, B.: Kinetics of pull-ups; overgrasp vs undergrasp. *Proc. Int'l Biomechanics Seminar,* Basel, S. Karger (in press).

16. Ricci, B., Mowatt, M., Dingle, R., Kent, J., and Mott, L.: Discriminatory power of the Harvard step-test. *Arbeitsphysiol.* (in press).

17. Tipton, C. M., and Karpovich, P. V.: Clinical electrogoniometry. *J. Phys. Ment. Rehab., 18*:90–95, 1964.

Chapter

7

REGULATORY MECHANISM: HEAT AND WATER LOSS

Preparation for this series of laboratory exercises is gained from the reading of Chapters 7, *Heat Regulation,* and 9, *Homeostasis of Body Fluids,* in *Physiological Basis of Human Performance* by B. Ricci (Philadelphia, Lea & Febiger, 1967).

The law of heat exchange influences man as well as inanimate objects. Heat, in energy form, is unidirectionally transferred from warmer to cooler substances.

Man takes heed of the law of heat exchange and as a result profits immeasurably, as evidenced by his versatility. Because he has learned to control his microclimate, he is able to explore the ocean depths, mountain tops, and the moon.

Man is a heat producer, heat production being a by-product of his ever-functioning biochemical activity.

His unique brain-centered thermoregulatory mechanism permits man to adjust to diverse climates. When in a cool environment, he automatically regulates his core temperature mainly by the radiation process. When this escape avenue is closed, as in a hot environment, another avenue is effectively utilized—evaporation of stored water.

When ambient conditions are unfavorable to evaporation, as when high temperature is accompanied by high relative humidity, water loss is ineffective in the maintenance of stable core temperatures. Unable to evaporate, the water (now called sensible perspiration) collects in droplets and rolls down the skin or is absorbed by the clothing. Changes in composition and specific gravity of perspiration reveal the ineffectiveness of this method of temperature control.

Analysis of yet another fluid, urine, reveals some insight into the effectiveness of temperature control as well as the level and condition of metabolic activity.

The level of metabolic activity is noted by monitoring and interpreting core and shell temperatures and water losses in the form of perspiration and urine.

Discussion

Man is a homeotherm.* Irrespective of wide changes in environmental temperature, sedentary man exhibits a rather narrow, cyclic change in core temperature. These cyclic changes are termed diurnal variations. When man becomes physically active, however, his core temperature reaches a level which, in comparison with sedentary readings, is febrile, yet normal for the situation. His physiological ability to withstand such periods of prolonged stress is dependent upon a number of factors which relate to temperature regulation, such as environmental conditions and physiological adaptability.

The term "environmental conditions" includes such interrelated considerations as ambient temperature, relative humidity, and suitability of clothing as well as wind and chill factors. Physiological adaptability relates primarily to neural control of core and shell temperatures, cardiovascular involvement including blood-shunting, and kidney involvement.

Irrespective of mechanism, the governing factor in heat exchange is that of temperature gradient: heat will be unidirectionally transferred—from warm to cool matter. Man's main avenues of heat loss are the processes of radiation and evaporation, the effectiveness of each process being related to environmental conditions. To the level of approximately equal temperatures between man and environment, heat *loss* through radiation is *inversely* related to environmental temperature. When the environmental temperature exceeds that of the body, heat is *gained* in *direct* relation to environmental temperature.

Evaporation of body water is another effective means of heat loss that is also dependent upon environmental conditions. High air temperature coupled with low relative humidity is most conducive to effective control of body temperature through vaporization of body water. Excluding extremes of air temperature, evaporation rate is inversely related to relative humidity.

Suitability of clothing relates primarily to texture and fit. Whether the articles worn by participants in physical activity should be snugly or loosely fitted or heavy or light textured depends upon environmental

---

* Also called "endotherm" and characterized by an ability to produce and regulate heat in contrast to poikilotherms (ectotherms) whose body temperatures fluctuate with environmental temperature.

conditions, intensity, and duration of metabolic activity, degree of acclimatization, and, in formal athletics, the requirements of the sport.

The classification of air velocity as pleasant or unpleasant or as beneficial or nonbeneficial to heat balance is related to environmental temperature. A comfort index, the equivalent chill temperature, has much
relevance for the military commander and should have relevance for the
athletics coach and outdoor construction foreman. Air temperature at
0° C feels cool if the wind velocity is zero; however if the wind velocity
is 20 km/h, the air seems very cold (see Table A–4 in the Appendix).

The rate of heat loss is controlled by the brain. Increase in core temperature resulting from increased metabolism induced by physical performance is slight. By comparison, shell temperatures are variable and
fluctuate as a function of exposure of the skin surface, insulating quality
of clothing, extent of surface vasodilatation and velocity of blood flow,
and rate of evaporation of perspiration. Blood shunting from kidney
vasoconstriction contributes to convection-radiation heat loss.

Although a small amount of heat is lost through micturition, attention
is directed to urine composition as an indicator of metabolic involvement
and extent of water loss. Copious water loss through evaporation is reflected by an increase in the density of urine.

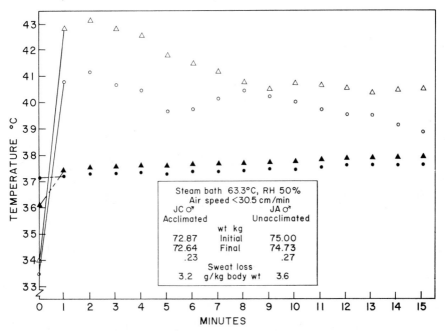

Fig. 7–1. Responses of an acclimated and an unacclimated individual to steam bath.
Subject JC represented by • T core and ○ T abdomen; JA by ▲ T core and △ T abdomen. Height of JC 166.4 cm, JA 185.9 cm.

Stress imposed upon individuals by high environmental temperature is manifested in a number of ways, notably by increases in core and shell temperature as well as in sweating rate reflected by accompanying weight loss. This is evident in Figure 7–1.

Acclimation and acclimatization have specific meanings. Acclimation is reserved for use in describing exposure to environmental chambers, whereas acclimatization describes exposure to an outdoor environment.

Laboratory Exercise Number 14—Heat Production and Avenues of Heat Loss during Exercise

(Read text pp. 141–150)

Required Apparatus and Materials*

Tele-thermometer, 6 channel, 0° to 51° C, including 6 probes: 1 physiological and 5 surface temperature
Clinical (oral) thermometer
Thermometer (−1 to 20° C)
Surgical tape,† roll: 12.7 mm × 4.57 m
Sling psychrometer (see p. 180 Appendix)
Physician's scale
Electric metronome (40–208 strokes/min)
2 Sweat shirts (see Fig. 7–2)
1 Sweat trousers
Bench—20.3 cm
Miscellaneous items
 200 cc alcohol 70%
 2 Towels
 Orange juice, frozen concentrate
 Thermos bottle, 2 qt.
 2 Small paper cups
 Gauze pads

Definition of Terms

The *Tele-thermometer* is powered by direct current. Each of the *probes* is essentially a thermocouple that is composed of two dissimilar metallic conductors fused together and incorporated into a circuit. Consequently, the elements essential to the operation of Ohm's law are present. Body heat energy is transformed into electric energy and the resulting thermo-electric current is directed through a sensitive galvanometer which is calibrated in degrees centigrade (or Fahrenheit). The magnitude of current flow is directly related to the temperature difference between the two dissimilar metallic conductors.

Rectal temperature, symbolized by T_r, is one measure of the *core* or deep-tissue temperature, whereas *shell* or *surface temperature* is a measure of skin temperature, T_s.

---

* For approximate cost and for suggested Tele-thermometer source, see Appendix B, page 199.
 † Blenderm, a product of 3M Company.

Bellows-effect is a fanning effect that is produced by the flapping of loosely fitted articles of clothing during physical performance.

The thin layer of air which is trapped between skin and clothing is termed the *microclimate. Ambient* refers to the medium surrounding the body; ambient temperature would refer to the temperature of the surrounding air.

Relative humidity, as descriptively implied, is a ratio of water vapor saturation to maximum possible saturation of volume of air. It is symbolized as RH and reported as a percentage. Wet-bulb and dry-bulb air temperature readings are recorded on hygrometers or sling psychrometers.

Body heat is lost mainly through *radiation,* i.e., through emitted infrared waves and through *vaporization* or *evaporation* of perspiration.* Small losses of body heat occur through convection, i.e., by the movement of heated air which rises from the body and is replaced *by* cooler air, and through *conduction*—via physical contact.

Procedure

1. Switch upper Tele-thermometer selector to "test" and lower selector to "probe 1." Needle should settle over red calibration line. If necessary, align needle with calibration index by turning adjustment screw (on lower right front panel). When the instrument is not being used, the lower switch should be turned to "off" position to prevent deterioration of batteries.

2. Place a small flap of adhesive tape near the end of the phone jack of each surface-temperature probe; number probes consecutively.

3. Prepare 1000 ml of orange juice and place in the freezer compartment of the refrigerator; stir the juice periodically until its temperature is approximately 1° C or slightly lower. Transfer juice to refrigerated compartment or pour into pre-cooled thermos bottle.

4. Determine relative humidity (see p. 180).

5. Subject prepares for laboratory exercise by donning one-legged sweat trousers and sweat shirt as shown in Figure 7–2.

    A. Subject inserts physiological probe 15.5 cm into his rectum.† Course the lead downward through undergarment then upward to one side of waist. NOTE: First establish 15.5-cm distance and mark with narrow, encircling strip of tape. If needed, petroleum jelly should be used *sparingly.*

    B. Attach the numbered surface temperature probes to the following areas:

        (1) Mid-medial left thigh (covered).

        (2) Mid-medial right thigh (exposed).

---

* Perspiration and sweat are synonymous.

† Optimum depth of insertion as noted by Mead and Bonmarito.[7]

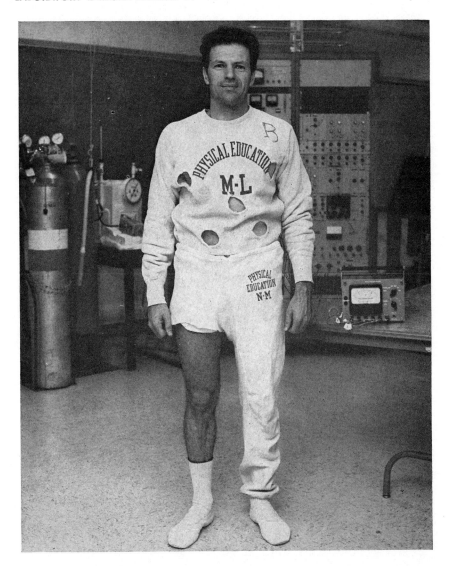

Fig. 7–2. Experimental shirt B and one-legged trousers. Note surface probe attached to mid-medial thigh. Note wires gathered to one side and fastened. Tele-thermometer is also pictured.

    (3) Chest: mid sternum (covered).
    (4) Calf: mid right calf belly (exposed).
    (5) Lower arm: mid-medial belly of forearm flexors (covered).
C. Insert numbered probe plugs into corresponding Tele-thermometer jacks; plug physiological probe into channel 6. Instruct sub-

Subject_____ Wt_____kg W_{TOT}_____kgm   Date_____

RH_____% T_{amb}_____°C

	Elapsed time, min.	Conventional Sweat Shirt							Experimental Sweat Shirt						
		T_{lt}	T_{rt}	T_{ch}	T_{cf}	T_{fa}	T_r	T_o	T_{lt}	T_{rt}	T_{ch}	T_{cf}	T_{fa}	T_r	T_o
Rest	5														
Work	2														
	4														
	6														
	8														
	10														
	ΣT														
	T̄														
Recovery	2														
	4														
	6														
	8														
	10														
	12														
	14														
	16														
	ΣT														
	T̄														

Data Sheet 7-1

ject to assume a sitting position and insert oral thermometer. Following a 5-minute rest interval, read and record all temperatures (see Data Sheet 7–1).

6. Record temperature of orange juice. Dispense juice to subject in small volumes. NOTE: Keep juice refrigerated or in thermos until subject is ready for another drink. Following ingestion of 1 liter of orange juice, take another set of readings including oral temperature.

7. Record weight of subject (in kilograms).

8. Subject performs 10-minute step-test on 20.3-cm bench at cadence of 25 complete steps/minute (set metronome at 100). Record all temperatures, except oral, every two minutes.

9. Following a 10-minute exercise bout, record core and surface temperatures every two minutes for 16 minutes; record oral temperature at end of exercise and at end of recovery period.

10. Instruct subject to dry off (with towel) before changing into the experimental sweat shirt (see Fig. 7–2). Establish new control values. Except for the ingestion of orange juice, repeat steps 7 and 8 above.

11. Subject is responsible for cleaning and sterilizing physiological probe with alcohol-moistened gauze pads. Surface probes should also be sterilized with alcohol.

Data Treatment

1. Plot the results of the first exercise bout. Express temperatures as a function of time. Indicate time of ingestion of cold orange juice by a small arrow along X axis.

2. Compare the effectiveness of each shirt by plotting mean skin temperature (work phase) as a function of time. Use Burton's[3] weighted skin temperatures:

$$\overline{T}_s = .50T_{ch} + .36T_{cf} + .14T_{fa}$$

where: ch = chest, cf = calf, and fa = forearm

3. Plot the mid-medial thigh temperature of the exposed thigh with $\overline{T}_s$ for *one* exercise bout. NOTE: In each assignment, be certain to indicate work accomplished and relative humidity as well as ambient temperature conditions.

Additional Notes

Exercise bouts conducted on a bicycle ergometer or treadmill can replace the step-test. Of importance, however, is the performance of equivalent work during each session in order that valid comparisons can be made of heat loss during each performance.

Burton's simple, weighted mean expression is suited to a laboratory exercise; however, as was shown by Teichner,[13] mean body surface temperature calculated from the Burton formula[3] does not correlate highly with a 10-point weighted mean. Yet, Teichner[13] noted the uncorrected temperature of one point—the mid-medial thigh—to estimate the weighted mean closely. This was corroborated by Ramanathan.[9]

Mean body temperature may also be expressed as a function of core and mean shell temperature. As advanced by Burton[3]

$$\overline{T}_{body} = 0.65\ T_r + 0.35\ T_s$$

Discussion Topics

1. Account for the differing surface temperatures between right and left thigh.

2. Relate sensible and insensible perspiration to physical activity performed by an unacclimatized person on a hot, humid day: 33° C, RH 85%, wind < 1 km/h.

3. As coach of the football, soccer, or field hockey team, what advice would you give your players relative to salt and water intake. Outline your talk.

4. Outline the relationship between cardiac failure and hot, humid weather.

Laboratory Exercise Number 15—Sweat Loss and Composition

(Read text pp. 145–150)

Required Apparatus and Materials.*

Tele-thermometer, 6-channel, 0–51° C, including 1 physiological probe and 5 surface temperature probes
Sling psychrometer (see Appendix p. 180)
Physician's scale
Electric metronome (40–208 strokes/min)
Cloth sweat shirt and trousers
Plastic (vinyl) sweat shirt and trousers
Surgical tape,† roll: 12.7 mm × 4.57 m
Hydrogen ion test paper, short-range comparators to span pH range 4.0 to 7.0
Bench 40.6 cm

Miscellaneous items

Gauze pads
2 Towels
200 cc alcohol, 70%

Definition of Terms

Reread "Definition of Terms" pp. 107–108.
Estimation of pH of perspiration and urine is easily accomplished by using litmus paper or sensitized *hydrogen ion test papers*. The pH value is determined by matching the strip color with a designated color chart.
The *plastic warm-up suit* consists of a plastic jersey or jacket and trousers which may be worn by athletes or by individuals attempting to "sweat off weight." It is nonabsorbent and is snugly fitted at the wrists, neck, and ankles.

Procedure

1. Prior to the laboratory session, the subject must evacuate bladder and bowels.
2. After subject inserts rectal probe to 15.5 cm, the numbered surface probes are attached to the following areas:

* For approximate cost, see Appendix B, page 200.
† Blenderm, a product of 3M Company.

A. Chest: mid-sternum.

B. Abdomen, midway between umbilicus and inferior sternum.

C. Approximately 10 cm below inferior angle of right scapula.

D. Approximately 10 cm below inferior angle left scapula.

3. Obtain nude weight of subject (with probes affixed); record weight. See Data Sheet 7–2.

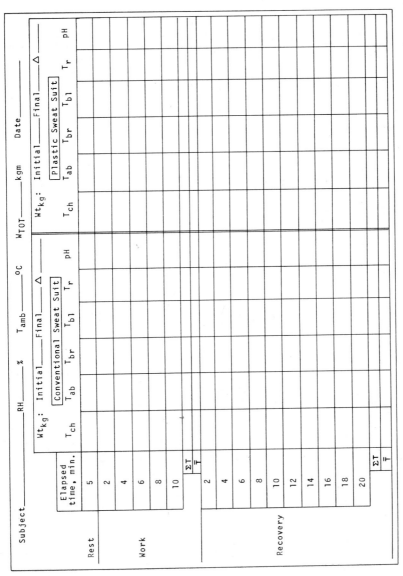

Data Sheet 7-2

4. Subject dons conventional sweat suit and assumes a sitting position. Insert numbered probes into corresponding Tele-thermometer jacks; plug physiological probe into channel 5. Following a five-minute rest interval, read and record all temperatures.

5. Place a strip of hydrogen ion test paper in contact with perspiration droplet in axilla; record pH.

6. Record ambient temperature and relative humidity (see p. 180).

7. Subject performs a 10-minute step-test on 40.6-cm bench at cadence of 20 completed steps/minute. Record all temperatures at two-minute intervals during exercise and continuing until twentieth minute of sitting recovery.

8. Determine pH of perspiration after 20-minute recovery period.

9. Subject thoroughly dries himself; once again nude weight is recorded.

10. Prepare for second work bout. If necessary, re-attach surface probes. Subject dons plastic suit. Repeat the above procedure.

11. NOTE: Subject is responsible for cleaning and sterilizing physiological probe with alcohol-dampened gauze pads. Clean surface probes with alcohol also.

Data Treatment

1. Compare the effectiveness of each garment relative to heat dispersal by portraying the mean anterior and mean posterior shell temperatures and core temperature as a function of time. Indicate the pH values on the graph. Note also the ambient temperature and relative humidity.

2. Calculate the kilocaloric cost of sweating: 1 g sweat = 0.58 kcal. NOTE: Estimation of sweat loss is based on weight loss.

Additional Notes

More dramatic results can be demonstrated by having the subject perform for longer work periods, e.g., 20 minutes at elevated ambient temperature and relative humidity. In addition to shell and core temperatures, telemetered cardiac frequency data would yield interesting, meaningful information that would reflect varying conditions of stress. Temperature- and humidity-controlled chambers and telemetering units, however, represent added financial outlay.

Should interest warrant, an inexpensive heat chamber could be constructed of clear, 4-mil plastic* draped over a wooden frame of desired size. Heat and humidity would be supplied by a pailful of water placed

---

* Available in widths from 3 to 40 feet (100-foot length); cost is nominal, ¾¢ per square foot per roll and 1½¢ per square foot per cut lengths. Source: Agway, Inc. (Farm Supplies).

on top of an electric heater within the "chamber." A small electric fan placed in an upper corner would circulate the hot, moist air. A thermometer and hygrometer would complete the apparatus requirement.

While convenient to use, the pH test strips yield coarse values. Colorimetric pH methods are more precise but, for example, are subject to errors introduced by temperature and concentration. Most precise determinations are obtained with pH meters.

Discussion Topics

1. Relate high ambient temperature and relative humidity to cardiac stress during exercise.

2. Discuss the physiological pros and cons of wearing plastic sweat suits during exercise.

3. Relate pH and specific gravity of sweat to water balance.

4. Relate acclimation to sauna or steam baths.

Laboratory Exercise Number 16—Effect of Exercise on Urine Volume and Composition

(See text pp. 212–213, also Fig. 8–6, p. 169)

Required Apparatus and Materials*

Urine specimen bottles, graduated
3 Urinometers, approx. 12-ml size
Hydrogen ion test papers, short-range comparators to span pH range 4.0 to 8.0
Reagent strips (Labstix), bottle (125)
Karo syrup, 1 pint
Distilled water, 1000 ml

Definition of Terms

A *urinometer* is a modified hydrometer which is used to measure the specific gravity of urine.

Specific gravity of urine is a measure of the density of the urine in comparison with that of distilled water.

The *pH* of urine relates to its degree of acidity or alkalinity.

The amount of sugar present in urine is determined by the glucose test. During a 24-hour period, approximately 1 gram of glucose is excreted, hence normal basal urine samples are expected to yield trace amounts of glucose. Postprandial samples may contain 0.25% glucose, which would reflect the intake of a fairly large amount of starch.

Another descriptive word, *proteinuria*, refers to the presence of proteins in urine—chiefly albumin but including lesser amounts of globulin. Normally, protein is present in trace amounts; however, excesses in the intake of protein, e.g., milk and eggs, serves to elevate the protein level in urine. An increase in the albuminuria level is also associated with prolonged periods of standing and is variously called "orthostatic" or "postural" proteinuria. An elevated albumin level also follows severe exercise and prolonged exposure to cold. Raised albumin levels are also noted during the pubertal state and during the menstrual period when serum albumin is introduced directly into the urine.

The presence of *ketones* in urine, notably acetone and acetoacetic acid, is called *ketonuria*. Being by-products of fat metabolism, ketones will be present in elevated amounts following high fat intake. Utilization and

---

* For approximate cost and for suggested Labstix source, see Appendix B, pp. 200–201.

destruction of adipose tissue, as during fasting states, will also result in above-normal amounts of ketones in the urine.

The presence of blood in urine, termed *hematuria,* is an abnormal finding. Hemoglobin may appear in the urine of normal persons following strenuous physical activity and sometimes after mild, prolonged activity. This condition is called *march hemoglobinuria.*

Basal urine sample refers to urine which is collected when the subject arises in the morning following 12 hours of abstinence from food, drugs, and water.

Procedure

1. Each student is to provide, and bring to the laboratory for analysis, a basal urine sample.

2. Determine and record the specific gravity of urine (see Data Sheet 7–3).

    A. Fill urinometer with the urine sample to within 1 cm of top. To prevent the formation of bubbles the urinometer should be *tilted* while the urine is being poured into it from the specimen jar.

    B. Obtain and record urine temperature.

    C. *Slowly introduce* the hydrometer into the *center* of the cylinder. Read the specific gravity at *eye level.* NOTE: To lessen the chances of error, remove foam from top of urine (scoop with filter paper), do *not* drop float into urine, and do not take the reading when the float adheres to side of cylinder.

    D. Note the temperature at which the hydrometer was calibrated and correct the specific gravity by *adding* or *subtracting* 0.0001 for each 3° C above or below the hydrometer calibrated temperature.

URINALYSIS

Subject_____   date _____

    Urine t°C_____   Hydrometer calib. t°C_____

Sp Gr$_{observed}$ —————————

Sp Gr$_{corrected}$ (Note: treat expression algebraically)

    = Sp Gr$_{obsvd}$ ± (Hydrometer t°C - Urine t°C) (0.0001 per 3°C diff)

    = _____

    glucose_____   ketones_____   pH_____
    protein_____   blood_____

Data Sheet 7-3

E. Remove hydrometer, *rinse* and *dry* it carefully and place it to one side.

3. Utilizing the appropriate reagent strips (Labstix), analyze urine for pH, glucose, protein, ketones, and blood.

4. Empty urinometers and rinse and place them (inverted) on rack.

5. Collect a control urine sample as well as a post-treatment sample from each of three subjects. For each sample, record specific gravity, pH, glucose, protein, ketones and blood levels (see Data Sheet 7–4).

A. Subject 1 is excused from the laboratory to jog for 30 minutes. He is not permitted to drink until a post-exercise sample has been collected.

B. Subject 2 will remain sedentary and is denied fluids.

C. Subject 3 will drink 1 liter of a sweetened drink consisting of 10% Karo syrup in distilled water.

Data Treatment

1. Calculate the mean and standard deviation and report the range of the basal urine samples for males and females separately.

2. Report in tabular form the analysis of control and post-treatment urine samples for the three subjects.

Additional Notes

Urine is formed at the approximate rate of 1 ml/minute. Assuming a sedentary role and heat balance, an increased fluid intake will serve as a diuretic. Other factors which contribute to diuresis include nervous influences (e.g., emotions) and prolonged exposure to cold. Decreased urine volume may reflect diminished fluid intake or increased rate of body fluid loss as during prolonged sweating.

Date____	Subject 1 Jogger			Subject 2 Sedentary			Subject 3 Sweetened Drink		
	Pre	Post	Δ	Pre	Post	Δ	Pre	Post	Δ
Sp Gr$_{corr}$									
pH									
Glucose									
Protein									
Ketones									
Blood									
Ambient Condition	RH____% t____°C			RH____% t____°C			RH____% t____°C		

Data Sheet 7-4

Urinalysis is easily accomplished with reagent strips. These strips are sensitive; however, care must be taken to avoid drawing conclusions from analysis of one or even several urine samples. Urinalysis must be considered in light of food intake and level of metabolic intensity.

It has been said that "Americans possess the richest urine in the world." Without doubt allusion was made to the ingestion of self-prescribed vitamins, tonics, and a host of so-called ergogenic aids which purport to restore vigor and recapture youth. Analysis of urine is revealing!

Discussion Topics

1. Enumerate and discuss the controls which must be established before validity can be structured into urine assay.

2. Relate sensible and insensible fluid loss to urine specific gravity.

3. Discuss in physiological terms the results of this laboratory exercise.

4. Relate electrolyte and water balance to urine pH and specific gravity.

Concluding Remarks

Man can tolerate heat and water imbalances; however, these imbalances are incurred at the price of reduced efficiency of physical performance.

Among other aptitudes, man is a heat producer as well as regulator of heat losses. The remarkably narrow core temperature fluctuation he exhibits during rest is evidence of his success in maintaining heat balance. Production is the result of biochemical activity; regulation, achieved primarily by radiational and evaporative means, is dependent upon environmental conditions and physiological adaptation.

Body temperature is reflected in both core and shell values.

As was noted by Mead and Bonmarito,[7] values vary with the depth at which the rectal probe is inserted. Within the rectum, movement of the probe to areas of differing densities, e.g., proximity to bone or muscle tissue, is also responsible for temperature variations.

Core temperature can also be reflected by tympanic membrane temperature. This technique, involving an earplug and thermocouple, was reported by Minard and Copman.[8]

Shell or surface temperature has also been expressed by the weighted mean technique. For the interested reader, the following sources are suggested: Burton,[2,3] Hardy and DuBois,[5] Hardy,[4] Teichner,[13] Ramanathan,[9] and Snellen.[12]

Body core and shell temperatures are also capable of being telemetered.

Thermography, the measurement of body heat which is emitted as infrared radiation, has been accomplished by the camera-scanner technique: the emitted infrared rays are optically collected, transformed into electrical impulses and amplified, and presented as a thermal image or thermogram. Film recorded temperatures can be read to $0.69°$ C (see Barnes[1]).

The estimation of sweat loss based on weight loss is one of the more simple techniques which is suited to laboratory use. A coarse estimate of the chemical composition of perspiration can be easily made with the use of indicating paper.

Additional methods of sweat measurement, as presented by Robinson and Robinson,[10] include: (1) microscopic examination of sweat droplets, (2) securing imprints on absorbent paper, (3) use of color indicators on the skin, (4) notation of changes in skin resistance as reflected by galvanic current, and (5) collection of water vapor from evaporated sweat. A detailed discussion of the chemical composition of sweat is also presented by Robinson and Robinson.[11]

By sartorial elegance criterion, designers of athletic uniforms are imaginative, but when heat balance is considered, they are unimaginative.

For football players, periodic change in helmet design has provided increased head protection, but ventilation has not been noticeably improved. Lighter shoulder pads have been produced, but they prevent heat loss by covering up large areas of the back and chest. Jerseys have undergone a metamorphosis from durable, heavy types to light, tear-away, short-sleeve types. The nylon mesh jersey has recently been introduced but its effectiveness remains to be measured. In the manufacture of jersies, effort should be directed toward improvement of air circulation by bellows effect or other means.

More effective teaching and performance can result from the application of knowledge gained from heat regulation and balance.

There is also the promise of preserving one's mental health in the postnuptial years by engaging in pre-marital experimentation in the temperature fluctuations of one's intended marriage partner to determine the degree of compatibility. Kleiber[6] suggests

> ". . . that two types of human beings may be distinguished by pattern of their temperature fluctuations during a day: the early risers and the late risers. The early risers have a relatively high body temperature in the morning and are barbarically cheerful before breakfast. The larger group are those who have difficulty in getting up in the morning and have unfriendly dispositions, at least until after the first cup of coffee. Their body temperature is low in the morning but high at night. Then they are wide awake while the early risers are tired and sleepy."

REFERENCES

1. Barnes, R. B.: Thermography of the human body. *Science, 140*:870–877, 1963.

2. Burton, A. C.: A new technic for the measurement of average skin temperature over surfaces of the body and the changes of skin during exercise. *J. Nutr., 7*: 481–496, 1934.

3. Burton, A. C.: Human calorimetry II. The average temperature of the tissues of the body. *J. Nutr., 9*:261–280, 1935.

4. Hardy, J. D.: Heat transfer. *In* Newburgh, L. H.: *Physiology of Heat Regulation and the Science of Clothing.* Philadelphia, W. B. Saunders Co., 1949.

5. Hardy, J. D., and DuBois, E. F.: Basal metabolism, radiation, convection, and vaporization at temperatures of 22 to 35° C. *J. Nutr., 15*:477–497, 1938.

6. Kleiber, M.: *The Fire of Life. An Introduction to Animal Energetics.* New York, John Wiley & Sons, 1961.

7. Mead, J., and Bonmarito, C. L.: Reliability of rectal temperatures as an index of internal body temperatures. *J. Appl. Physiol., 2*:97–109, 1949.

8. Minard, D., and Copman, L.: Elevation of body temperature in health. *In* Hardy, J. D. (Ed.): *Biology and Medicine,* vol. 3, part 3. *Temperature: Its Measurement and Control in Science and Industry.* New York, Reinhold Publishing Corp., 1963.

9. Ramanathan, N. L.: A new weighting system for mean surface temperature of the human body. *J. Appl. Physiol., 19*:531–533, 1964.

10. Robinson, S., and Robinson, A. H.: Measurement of sweating. *In* Steele, S. M.: *Methods in Medical Research.* Chicago, Year Book Publishers, Inc., 1954.

11. Robinson, S., and Robinson, A. H.: Chemical composition of sweat. *Physiol. Rev., 34*:202–220, 1954.

12. Snellen, J. W.: Mean body temperature and the control of sweating. *Acta Physiol. Pharmacol. Neerl., 14*:99–174, 1966.

13. Teichner, W. H.: Assessment of mean body surface temperature. *J. Appl. Physiol., 12*:169–176, 1958.

Chapter

8

ASSESSING RESPIRATORY VOLUMES*

Laboratory preparation involves the reading of Chapter 6, *Respiration*, as well as pages 247 (footnote), 250–256, and 292, in *Physiological Basis of Human Performance* by B. Ricci (Philadelphia, Lea & Febiger 1967).

Man walks at the bottom of an "ocean" of air. At regular intervals during each minute of his entire life span he draws in a small quantity of air, and moments later exchanges this volume for another. This act does not tax his thought process for it is involuntary. Thus, man is able to shut out thought processes and engage in such required activities as sleep without having to worry about meeting his incessant demand for air.

The flow of gas to and from the lungs is called respiration. It is an indispensable function which man performs in common with all living animals.

Discussion

Respiration consists of inhalation and exhalation. This exchange of gases between atmosphere and lungs—the external phase of respiration—is the result of physical-chemical-neural involvement.

Irrespective of the type of involvement, the ultimate mechanism which effects inhalation-exhalation is physical in nature. Gases seek equilibrium. Any differences between gas pressure of the ambient air (or source gas) and that of the gas within the lungs will be rectified by a movement of the gases from the area of greater pressure to that of lesser pressure until equilibrium is attained.

* NOTE: It is assumed that participants in these laboratory exercises are free of upper respiratory tract or lung infections. Under these conditions, 70% alcohol solution is suitable as a sterilizing agent for mouthpieces. If, for example, the determination of the respiratory function of tubercular or emphysematous patients is contemplated, the reader is urged to consult with a medical technologist in order to obtain a more effective germicidal.

123

The lungs are contained within an osseo-cartilaginous-muscular enclosure that is capable of changing its shape and therefore, its internal capacity. Enclosing the bottom portion of the thorax is the involuntary diaphragm muscle. While it descends, as during inhalation, it effects a pressure disequilibrium. The air within the lungs is now capable of occupying a larger volume (owing to the reduced pressure exerted by the descended diaphragm) and it exerts a reduced pressure. Thus, the flow of gases is favorable from the ambient air into the lungs. The process is reversed as the diaphragm ascends during exhalation.

Lung tissue, although extensible, is passive. The contiguous layers of moist lung and thoracic tissue constitute an ideal setting for the occurrence of molecular attraction; each time the rib cage is elevated the lungs expand. The gas molecules, now occupying a larger area within the lungs, become less compressed, hence, exert reduced pressure. Air moves into the lungs until pressure equilibrium is attained. Rhythmically and alternately, the process is reversed.

Demonstrating the role of the diaphragm muscle by means of the bell jar* is effective in that the results of pressure differences caused by the movement of the rubber membrane are readily observed. The balloons, representing the lungs, inflate and deflate as the membrane is lowered and raised. Yet, this presentation must be viewed with caution because it fails to demonstrate the *simultaneous* excursions of the chest wall which contribute significantly to external respiration. It is important to visualize the diaphragm lowering simultaneously as the chest wall raises and the diaphragm raising simultaneously as the chest wall lowers. Movement within the thorax is multidimensional.

Carbon dioxide exerts a profound effect on ventilation. This is accomplished in one of two ways: (1) by decreasing the carbon dioxide tension or (2) by increasing the carbon dioxide content of inspired air. The principal, natural regulatory mechanism is provided by decreased blood carbon dioxide tension which stimulates the respiratory center. The second mechanism, that of increasing the carbon dioxide content of inspired air, is used advantageously by the practical physician who, when the occasion indicates such action, throws a paper bag over his athlete-patient's head in order to restore normal breathing by means of the stimulating effect produced by the rebreathing of elevated, exhaled carbon-dioxide levels.

Often overlooked is the regulatory role of ventilation by oxygen. This mechanism was elucidated by Nobel Laureate Heymans who discovered,

---

* Bell jar (a bottomless gallon jar will suffice) is closed at its top by a rubber stopper through which a glass Y tube passes (representing the trachea). A rubber membrane (representing the diaphragm muscle) extends over its base. Balloons (lungs) are secured to the ends of the Y tube within the jar.

within the aorta and carotid arteries, chemoreceptors which are sensitive to oxygen tension as well as to carbon dioxide tension.

Reflex control of ventilation has been elucidated. Gray,[3] noting the effect on ventilation of many contributing factors, proposed his *multiple factor theory.*

Because the quantity of gas varies with temperature and pressure, comparisons of gas volumes become meaningful only if standard conditions of measurement are universally adopted. STPD represents such an adoption of standard conditions for dry gas volumes at standard temperature (0° C) and standard pressure (760 mm Hg).

Within the lungs, however, gas is laden with moisture. When exhaled into a spirometer, the gas passes through a carbon dioxide absorber which is also a desiccant, hence, the moisture in the gas is removed. In addition, the temperature of the gas is usually reduced by approximately 15° C (from 37° C). Under these conditions the volume collected in the spirometer is reduced and is therefore not representative of the volume exchanged or of the volume within the lungs. Thus, the values are in need of correction, and, in this instance, the correction factor is represented by BTPS (body temperature, pressure, saturated with water).

BTPS is the appropriate correction factor to be used for all lung volumes calculated in this series of laboratory exercises.

Note from the BTPS formula (text p. 279) that 273° K, 37° C, and 47 mm Hg are constants. Note particularly that 47 mm Hg is the water vapor tension at 37° C (body temperature).

Orders for chart paper of special design for recording spirometers are cheerfully received and promptly dispatched by the manufacturer; however, reliance in the subsequent laboratory exercises will be on the "workhorse" formula for determining the volume of a cylinder: $V = \pi r^2 h$. Bell factor (the product of πr^2) is a mathematical expression which is utilized in the conversion of vertical displacements to volumes (see footnote, text p. 247). It is thoughtfully provided by the manufacturer and is stamped on the spirometer. Obviously, bell factors will vary inversely with cylinder size. Thus, the bell factor of a 350-liter gasometer will be much less than that of a 9-liter respirometer. Bell factors are expressed in cc/mm—cubic centimeters occupied per each millimeter displacement.

A spirometer which is devoid of carbon dioxide absorber and thermometer should not be used because it serves merely to compound error and does not allow for volume correction to BTPS. The effects of carbon dioxide on ventilation have been shown. (See text p. 90 and Fig. 5–6 p. 91. Also, read discussion on spirometer calibration, pp. 11–13.)

A barometer, or air pressure meter, is an essential laboratory item; pressure is expressed in mm Hg units. Increasingly noticeable, however, is the reporting of pressure in torr units—in recognition of Evangelista

Torricelli, the inventor of the mercury barometer.* For practical purposes, *torr*, an international standard term, is equal to 1 mm Hg pressure,† hence, in a laboratory exercise such as this one, the student is permitted to report P_B in torrs.

Finally, the reader is advised to comprehend the terminology and symbols relating to lung volumes and capacities (see text p. 114). In addition, he is asked to study the comparison of schema with spirogram (see text p. 115).

---

* An interesting historically documented tidbit follows: Torricelli, a pupil of Galileo, made his discovery in 1643. About three years later, Otto von Guericke (mayor of Magdeburg) invented a water barometer. Still later, Blaise Pascal invented a barometer which, as the reader has probably surmised, the "true" Frenchman filled with wine. Consider density: Torricelli's tube was short (probably not greater than 0.80 m), von Guericke's was 10.36 m, but Pascal's was high—with wine—14.02 m.

† Actually, to within 1 part in 5,000,000. Torr $= 1,013,250$ dynes/cm².

Laboratory Exercise Number 17—Subdivisions of Lung Volume Taken in the Erect Standing Position
(See text pp. 114–116, footnote p. 247, pp. 250–252, 292)

Required Apparatus and Materials*

Recording spirometer with 3-speed kymograph
Barometer, mercurial
Nose clips
Mouthpiece, rubber
Oxygen, USP (300 cu ft cylinder)
Regulator
Alcohol, 70% solution

Definition of Terms

A *recording spirometer* consists essentially of a kymograph and a movable bell, or cylinder, which is in constant contact with a water seal. A counter weight-pulley arrangement allows for an even excursion of the bell and reduces inertia. Located within the cylinder base is a canister containing granules which absorb carbon dioxide. (These granules also act as a desiccant.) (See Fig. 8–2, text p. 162.)

Bell factor is synonymous with πr^2 (of the bell or cylinder) and is expressed in cc/mm (see p. 125).

Two-stage vital capacity is the measure of inspiratory reserve volume and expiratory reserve volume in steps which are separated by normal breathing. Separation of the inhalation and exhalation phases by normal breathing characterizes the two-stage technique. It is *not* to be confused with two successive inhalations followed by two successive exhalations.

Procedure

1. Determine the barometric pressure (see p. 177).
2. Enter initials and sex of subject as well as position and date on data sheet. (See Data Sheet 8–1; convenient paper size is 28 × 43.3 cm.)
3. Ready the spirometer:
   A. Check the water level; keep water level at midpoint of gauge or approximately 2 cm from top.

* For approximate cost and for suggested recording spirometer source, see Appendix B, page 201.

Name_____

date   position

Spirogram

V_T _____

IRV_____

IC_____

ERV_____

VC_____

f/min_____

gas t °C_____

P_B _____

paper speed_____

Ventilogram

MV_____

f/min_____

V_T _____

gas t °C_____

P_B _____

paper speed_____

Fast tracing

F.E.V.$_{1.0}$" _____

paper speed_____

Data Sheet 8-1

B. Make certain that the spirometer is level. Take special note that the bell does not touch the cylinder housing at any level of its range. If necessary, manipulate the adjusting knobs at the corners of the base.

C. Connect the kymograph motor to the 115V alternating-current source.

D. Place the pen in the holder, which monitors the excursions of the bell, then fill it with ink.*

E. Secure the paper to the drum, being certain to overlap it properly. On drums which revolve in a *counterclockwise* direction be certain to place the left flap *under* the right one. This

---

* Orifice will not become clogged if the pen is rinsed with water at the conclusion of each laboratory session and is stored in an inverted position on a paper towel. This practice will eliminate the tedious and time-consuming task of boring the orifice with a fine wire.

eliminates the problem of the pen becoming caught in the flap, resulting in a torn tracing and possible pen damage.

F. Fill the spirometer with oxygen then determine if all valves are closed.

G. *Establish a short reference line* either by physically revolving the drum or by engaging the kymograph motor. NOTE: Because all measurements of displacement are drawn *perpendicular to a parallel base line,* the importance of a reference line cannot be underestimated (see Fig. 8–1).

4. Secure the nose clip to subject; instruct subject to attach mouthpiece to apparatus. NOTE: Ideally, the subject should face *away* from the bell. If this is not possible, place or suspend a shield between subject and bell. This reduces the possibility of aberrant spirograms.

5. Start the drum—at speed of 32 mm/min.

6. Instruct the subject to grasp the inner lip of the mouthpiece between his teeth and close his lips gently but firmly around the mouthpiece.

7. Open the two-way valve (to which the mouthpiece is attached). Subject is now breathing oxygen from the bell.

8. Allow subject to breathe normally for approximately three minutes, then instruct him to perform on command:

A. "Inhale maximally, return to normal breathing." When subject

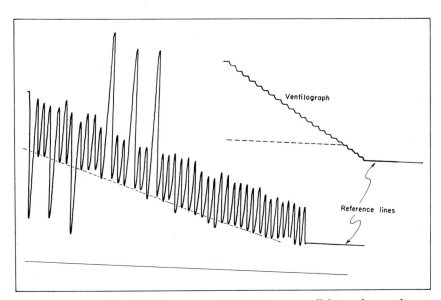

Fig. 8–1.   Base line (solid lowermost line) is drawn parallel to reference line at arbitrary location dictated by convenience. Broken line on ventilograph tracing is also parallel to reference line. Measurement of ERV, V_T, and IC are taken from sloped broken line depicted on spirogram which is established by eyeballing technique.

has attained normal breathing pattern (as reflected by spirogram), repeat the same procedure. At least three maximal inhalations should be recorded.

   B. While observing the spirogram, the operator must time his command "exhale maximally" to correspond with the *down swing*
of the pen, i.e., during the normal exhalation phase. NOTE: *Do
not allow* the subject to inhale before exhaling as this practice
may erroneously elevate the expiratory reserve values. At least
three maximal exhalations should be recorded.

9. The operator is further responsible for:
   A. Guaranteeing a correctly sloped spirogram. The counterclockwise drum movement results in a tracing from *right* to *left*. Because of the change in gas volume (caused by the subject's oxygen consumption) the spirogram will slope left upward. A slope
which is left downward (indicating an introduction of air into
the bell) is usually caused by a loose noseclip or an improperly
held mouthpiece.
   B. Reading and recording the gas temperature within the bell.
   C. Switching off the drum.
   D. Closing off the oxygen line by turning two-way valve (see 7
above).
   E. Advising subject when spirogram is completed, then handing
him a paper towel (to collect saliva).
   F. Instructing the subject to:
      (1). Rinse mouthpiece in tap water, then, using tongs,
      (2). dip mouthpiece into a beaker containing 70% alcohol solu-
         tion, or other effective germicide, and place on paper towel
         to air-dry.

10. Repeat procedural steps 4 to 9 for each subject. Also, replace the
source gas upon completion of the fifth spirogram.

11. Following the completion of the last spirogram, the student operator must:
   A. Remove and wash complete valve with a mild detergent then
rinse it and allow it to air-dry. NOTE: Stopcock grease must be
applied to the plug before the valve is reassembled.
   B. Disconnect the inlet-outlet tubing to allow air-drying.
   C. Rinse and store the pen (see footnote on p. 128).

12. If the spirometer is used for many subjects or for extended periods
the following additional steps should be taken to combat excessive moisture accumulation.*

---

* With soda-lime crystals the barium hydroxide lime reacts with the moisture and
carbon dioxide in the exhaled air to form additional moisture which contributes to the
efficiency of the absorber.

A. Raise bell completely out of water.

B. Remove absorber cannister as well as duck-bill valve.

C. NOTE: Check the condition of the granules and replace as required. Baralyme* granules contain an indicator which eliminates doubt: purple granules are spent and in need of replacement.

Data Treatment

1. See text pages 250–252. Each subject must calculate the following: V_T, IRV, IC, ERV, VC, and MV. Correct all values to BTPS. Note the following interrelationships: :

$$VC = IRV + V_T + ERV$$
$$VC = IC + ERV$$
$$(IC = IRV + V_T)$$

2. Calculate IRV, then ERV, as a percent of VC.

Additional Notes

More precise estimations will result if each student is allowed a period of time to conquer the distress of self-consciousness and to become acquainted with the "feel" of the apparatus, the nose clips, mouth-breathing, and the mouth-drying effect of the gas. These objectives might be accomplished during the week preceding this laboratory assignment.

More precise spirograms are assured if the student is prevented from watching the excursions of the bell—some individuals are adept at controlling the bell's amplitude.

Vital capacity values may reflect the many factors that influence them. Familiarization with assessment technique and with apparatus use represent two of the more widely accepted factors. Insistence on a stated posture is sometimes over-looked, e.g., vital capacity in a standing position will be greater by approximately 10% than that monitored from a sitting position.

Discussion Topics

1. What is meant by effective tidal volume? What is your effective V_T?

2. What do you imagine to be the effect on tidal volume of an arms-extended-overhead position? Why is this so?

3. Relate the importance of vital capacity to physical performance. Document your answers.

4. What effect does oxygen inhalation have on vital capacity?

* Baralyme is produced by National Cylinder Gas, Division of Chemetron Corporation, 840 North Michigan Avenue, Chicago, Illinois 60611.

Laboratory Exercise Number 18—Vital Capacity: One-Stage, Two-Stage, Timed, Predicted. Comparisons of Minute Volume Measurement

(See text pp. 250–256)

*Required Apparatus and Materials**

Same requirement as for Laboratory Exercise Number 17 as well as:
Stadiometer (on physician's scale)
Shoulder breadth caliper

Definition of Terms

Reread preceding "Definition of Terms" (p. 127).

One-stage vital capacity is the measure of the maximum volume of air which is exhaled following maximal inhalation. By comparison, *two-stage vital capacity* involves several maximal inhalations interspersed with intervals of normal breathing and followed by several maximal exhalations which are also interspersed with intervals of normal breathing.

While the two-stage technique is superior to the one-stage, both may be criticized because of the lack of a common time base. Standardization of times is desirable but this must first be carefully studied then subjected to experimentation.

There is available a technique which provides a common time base and thus makes comparisons between subjects valid. This technique is appropriately called the *timed capacity*. Following maximal inhalation, a tracing of the maximal exhalation is obtained. Actually, several successive tracings are obtained. Utilizing the fast drum speed, one-second volume is represented by the area under the curve formed by the tracing, a line extended from the initial indication of forceful exhalation (exhibiting perpendicularity to the reference line), and a base line representing one-second linear displacement of the drum (see Fig. 8–2). This is symbolized by $VC_{T\,1.0''} = F.E.V._{.1.0''}$; however, timed vital capacity is obviously not synonymous with forced *inspiratory* volume which is represented by the area under the upward slope of the curve.

As is implied in the term, *predicted vital capacity* is the estimated capacity of the lungs predicted from stature and mathematical constants.

As was noted in the previous laboratory exercise, calculation of minute volume from tidal volume (and respiration frequency/minute) is less than precise. The slope of the base line is guesstimated, by eyeballing,

---

* For approximate cost, see Appendix B, page 201.

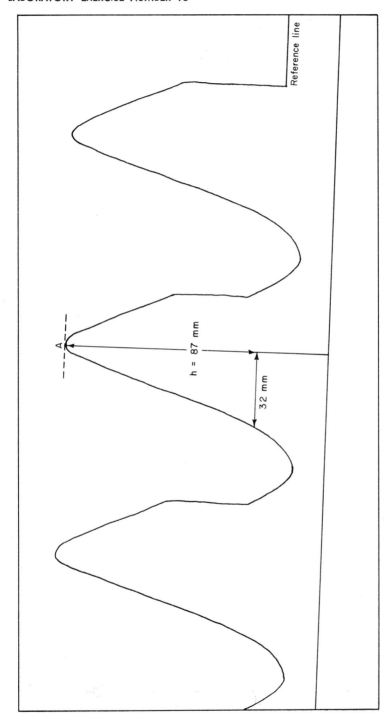

Fig. 8–2.   Fast tracing. Paper speed 1920 mm /min ∴ 32 mm/sec.   Several fast tracings can be obtained if the drum motor is switched off after each maximal exhalation phase has been completed.

in the hope that it "averages out the errors." The area defined by the ventilograph tracing with its linear and vertical displacement lines removes the element of guesstimation. (See Fig. 11–4, text p. 251.)

Calculation of tidal volume is accomplished by rearrangement of the formula for minute volume. The *ventilogram* is made possible by the inclusion of a second pen attached to a reduction gear-clutch mechanism

Fig. 8–3A.   Shoulder breadth caliper used in measurement of stem height. Caliper is placed in slotted portion of baseboard which is placed on top of bench.

which permits compact cumulative monitoring of the inhalation phase of ventilation. This "reduced" tracing must be multiplied by the gear reduction ratio which varies with each ventilograph head and is imprinted on the spirometer.

Stem height is the measure of trunk length from the ischial tuberosities to the suprasternal notch. It is conveniently taken from the sitting position (see Fig. 8–3A, B).

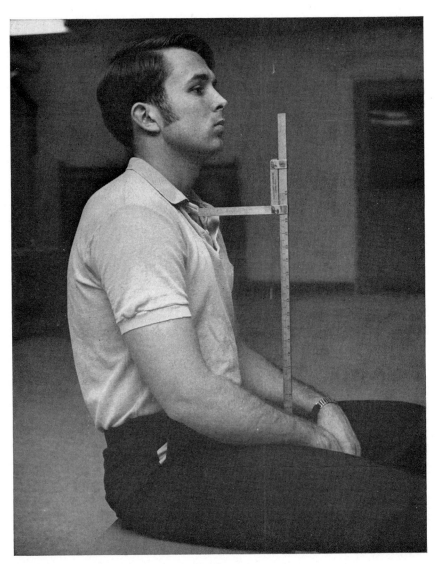

Fig. 8–3B.   Measurement of stem height.

10

Procedure

Follow the procedural steps listed on pages 127–131 with these additions:

1. Utilize *both* pens.

2. Adjust ventilograph pen to a position approximately 4 cm *above* bell pen by gently pulling out the clutch plate on pulley and rotating it clockwise to lower it.

3. Also, measure and record:

    A. Stature (in cm).

    B. Stem height (in cm) taken in the sitting position (see Fig. 8–3B).

4. During an uninterrupted interval, obtain the following spirograms in the order indicated (standing position):

    A. Utilizing *both* pens, obtain tracings of normal breathing. At the end of the third minute (approximately) discontinue the ventilograph by tilting the pen away from the drum.

    B. Command subject to "inhale maximally, exhale forcefully and maximally." Obtain several of these one-stage vital capacity tracings.

    C. Allow subject to breathe normally for approximately three minutes then instruct him to perform on command:

        (1). "Inhale maximally, return to normal breathing." When subject has attained normal breathing pattern (as reflected by spirogram), repeat the same procedure. At least two maximal inhalations should be recorded.

        (2). While observing the spirogram, the operator must time his command "exhale maximally" to correspond with the *down swing* of the pen, i.e., during the normal exhalation phase. NOTE: *Do not allow* the subject to inhale before exhaling. At least two maximal exhalations should be recorded.

    D. Stop drum, flip pen back, close by-pass valve below mouthpiece, then note and record gas temperature.

5. Turn data sheet over and establish a new reference line. Prepare to obtain a *fast tracing* as follows:

    A. Instruct subject to follow command: "inhale maximally, exhale forcefully and deeply." NOTE: The success of this fast tracing is assured if:

        (1). The operator times the flipping of the fast-speed switch (1920 mm/min) to coincide with the *nearly completed* inhalation phase. Several fast tracings can be obtained if the drum is switched off after the completion of each maximal

exhalation (see Fig. 8–2). Note: Allow subject to rest between tracings (while still attached to the spirometer).

(2). The subject exhales maximally and fully. Fast exhalations
can be expected to be less than maximal.

B. Stop drum (see 4D above); however, before allowing subject
to leave, the operator should eyeball the fast tracing to be
certain that the slope of the forced expiratory volume has tra-
versed a linear distance of at least 32 mm.

6. Obtain similar tracings for each subject.

Data Treatment

1. Calculate and correct to BTPS:
   A. VC both one-stage and two-stage.
   B. MV from spirogram and ventilogram.
   C. F.E.V.$_{1.0}$
2. Predicted VC (see formula, text p. 252).
3. Calculate the coefficient of correlation between stem height and
lung capacity (two-stage) for each laboratory population.
4. Express one-stage VC as a percentage of two-stage VC.
5. Express F.E.V.$_{1.0''}$ as a percentage of two-stage VC.
6. Express two-stage VC as a percentage of VC predicted.
7. Express MV (from ventilogram) in relation to BSA.

Additional Notes

Reliable measures are the outcome of thorough preparation for the
laboratory exercises. These include the use of a period of exposure to
the apparatus as well as the mastery of procedural steps.

Through proper organization, apparatus "idle time" can be kept to a
minimum thus assuring blocks of laboratory time which can be used to
complete the necessary mathematical calculations.

As one subject's spirogram nears completion, another subject should be
ready—with nose clip affixed and mouthpiece in hand—to take his prede-
cessor's place at the apparatus.

Stem height and stature measurements as well as calculation of predicted vital capacity can be accomplished during the interval of "waiting
for the apparatus."

The slide rule is a time and work saver, provided mastery has been
achieved. Expending inordinate amounts of time for simple calculations
is symptomatic of the need to practice. Exclusive of calculating the coefficient of correlation, all calculations required for this laboratory exercise should be completed within 30 minutes—a generous time allowance.

The integrity of a spirometer is related to the efficiency of its carbon dioxide absorber; however, obtaining the suggested tracings for this session by a class of thirty would not impair the efficiency of the absorber.

Discussion Topics

1. How does vital capacity relate to stem height?
2. Assuming that your actual vital capacity exceeds your predicted vital capacity, enumerate the factors which contribute to this. Based on some of your factors, can you relate this seemingly beneficial condition to fitness?
3. Are large vital capacity and low utilization coefficients possible? Why?
4. Are "respiratory gymnastics" beneficial? Document your answers.

Laboratory Exercise Number 19—Effect of Various Gas Mixtures on External Respiration

Required Apparatus and Materials*

Same requirement as for Laboratory Exercise Number 17 (p. 127) plus the following:
Carbon dioxide cylinder (60-lb.), purity 99.5%
Regulator

Definition of Terms

The success of this laboratory exercise is dependent upon the manner in which the gas mixture is administered, for if the subject were cognizant of the gas composition, a psychogenic effect would be introduced.

Three gas mixtures will be utilized and the order of administration will be *rotated*,† i.e., while each subject will breathe from all three mixtures, the order of administration may be different for successive subjects. Six different orders are possible (see p. 140).

In a non-operational sense, this may be termed a *single blind* technique in that only the subject is unaware of the specific mixture he is breathing. Incidentally, the term *single blind* has not been adopted by convention.

Control value refers to the value which serves as a basis for comparison of subsequent values.

Procedure

1. The following mixtures will be used:
   A. Oxygen (100%).
   B. Atmospheric air (79.04% N_2, 0.03% CO_2, 20.93% O_2).
   C. Oxygen (95%) and carbon dioxide (5%).
   NOTE: Only the instructor or his designee should introduce the mixture into the spirometer and should determine the sequence of source gas administration. This can be done in a number of ways with varying degrees of statistical purity—from pulling sequences out of a hat (random selection) to arbitrarily establishing the sequence as:

---

* For approximate cost, see Appendix B, page 202.
† By this technique, fatigue-effect is least likely to affect the results. This technique is *not* to be confused with the random selection technique of establishing sequence of mixture or selection of samples (subjects) of a population. Random selection characterizes sound experimental design, but is not applicable to this situation because the sample is biased by the fact that students are assigned (through convenience) to a laboratory section.

Subject	Sequence
1st	ABC
2nd	ACB
3rd	BAC
4th	BCA
5th	CAB
6th	CBA
7th and subse- quent subjects	Repeat order

Whatever the order, it must *not* be made known to the subject *until all spirograms have been completed.*

2. Follow procedural steps 1 through 6 (pp. 127–129) and 8 (p. 129); however, utilize ventilograph as well (see p. 136). *Sitting* position will be used throughout. Allow subject to breathe normally for four minutes. The derived calculations will serve as control values.

3. Release subject from spirometer.

4. Operator will introduce mixture A, B, or C according to the previously established sequence. *Do not allow any subject to view the introduction of source gas.* Obtain three additional spirograms each of four minutes' duration.

5. Upon completion of *all* spirograms (four per subject), notify each subject of his sequence of source gas.

6. Comply with steps 11 and 12 (p. 130).

Data Treatment

1. See text pages 250–252. Calculate the following on each of the four drawings: MV, respiration freq/min, V_T from ventilogram. NOTE: Use last full minute for calculations. Correct all values to BTPS.

2. Calculate, for each sex, the means and standard deviations of V_T, MV, and respiration freq/min resulting from control gas plus each of the gas mixtures.

3. Plot $\overline{V}_T$ and standard deviation as a function of gas composition. Depict females by a closed dot (•) and males by an X. Do likewise for $\overline{MV}$ and standard deviation.

Additional Notes

The carbon dioxide content of control gas and "gas" A is of trace proportion and is negligible in mixture B (approximately 0.03%). Initially, at 5%, the carbon dioxide content of mixture C will be reduced as a function of time because of the action of the carbon dioxide absorber in the spirometer. The exact carbon dioxide content remaining in the sample at the cessation of the spirogram can easily be determined through analysis (see pp. 168–171); however, it can be assumed that the content is reduced because of the presence of the carbon dioxide absorber.

A *double blind* approach may be used. In this instance, mixtures A, B, and C, prepared in advance, are re-coded P Q R or X Y Z by the instructor. Thus, the instructor's designee, unaware of the precise composition, merely dispenses the X, Y, or Z mixture; the gas composition in each cylinder is known only to the instructor. There are variations to this double blind approach. The subject and instructor's designee may be told only that "each of the cylinders contains gas mixtures which are *not* detrimental to health." In fact, the composition of each mixture may be the same or diverse and would depend upon the purpose of the laboratory exercise or upon the hypothesis. Whatever the format, the double blind approach solves the bias problem which can plague the research effort.

Subjects cannot detect differences between mixtures A, B, and C. These gases "taste" the same and each produces a "mouth-drying effect." Not to be overlooked, however, is the *power of suggestion.* Some subjects can become "dizzy" or "light-headed" on pure oxygen because they imagine themselves to be breathing "that high carbon dioxide gas"; they may so "inform" their colleagues.

Discussion Topics

1. What can you conclude from a comparison of the breathing patterns exhibited in the four spirograms? Use group data.

2. Discuss the chemical role in ventilation.

3. What probable effects would you expect from a mixture composed of 50% oxygen and 50% nitrogen? Document your answer.

4. Define *break point* and relate it to athletic performance.

Concluding Remarks

Some professional journals reflect a bountiful harvest of articles which relate pulmonary capacity or function to the physically active as well as inactive. Undoubtedly, major impetus was provided by the relatively low cost of apparatus (the apparatus became available to many) and by the ease of measurement.

Unfortunately, some of the least expensive spirometers* (costing less than $125.00) consist essentially of a chain compensated bell and single inlet tube. These can be used only for one-stage vital capacity assessment. More startling is the compounding of error resulting from bell excursion which is accompanied by much friction and inertia. Most inexcusable is the use of apparatus which beguiles the user, for without corrections for gas temperature and barometric pressure, vital capacities of Denverites will exceed the capacities of the Chattanoogans.

Comparisons of vital capacity, even though corrected to BTPS, lack meaning unless (1) capacity is related to body size, e.g., to stem height or body surface area and to age and sex, and (2) a common time base is established.

Clinical appraisal of pulmonary function has taken a giant forward leap. As pointed out by Comroe and co-workers,[1] "The study of pulmonary physiology has moved in one decade from the pure research laboratory into the hospital cardiopulmonary laboratory, the clinic, and the physician's office." Screening tests have evolved from pulmonary research. The work of Gaensler[2] is notable: normal individuals can be expected to exhale at least 75% of their vital capacity in one second.

Emphasis in this section has been placed upon the external phase of respiration. When the external phase is considered in relation to the internal phase, the results become more meaningful. These are discussed in the following chapter.

REFERENCES

1. Comroe, J. H., Foster, R. E., Dubois, A. B., Briscoe, W. A., and Carlsen, E.: *The Lung. Clinical Physiology and Pulmonary Function Tests,* 2nd Ed. Chicago, Year Book Medical Publishers, Inc., 1962.

2. Gaensler, E. A.: Analysis of ventilatory defect by timed capacity measurements. *Amer. Rev. Tuberc.,* 64:256–278, 1951.

3. Gray, J. S.: The multiple factor theory of the control of respiratory ventilation. *Science, 103:*739–744, 1946.

* The precise word is *exhalometer.* By comparison, *spirometers* allow for *rebreathing* of source gas.

9

ASSESSING METABOLIC FUNCTION: INDIRECT CALORIMETRY*

Preparation for the following series of laboratory exercises is achieved through the reading and comprehension of Chapter 8, *Metabolism,* and the rereading of pages 129–138 in Chapter 6, *Respiration,* in *Physiological Basis of Human Performance,* by B. Ricci (Philadelphia, Lea & Febiger, 1967).

Pollutants, warns the ecologist, could alter the gas composition of the atmosphere. Admittedly slow, the process involves the decimation of the oxygen producers—trees, shrubs, plant life in lakes, seaweeds—by the indiscriminate use of insecticides and herbicides and is complicated by the requirements of a runaway population and by the formation of hydrocarbons and other products of combustion. The time table has not been formulated; however, "we must do something before it is too late" is heard and read daily.

Of the air man presently breathes, the element of supreme importance to him constitutes but one fifth of the atmospheric mixture; however, man is versatile. He has demonstrated a capability of breathing pure oxygen. He has also demonstrated a capacity to perform scuba diving with gas mixtures containing small amounts of oxygen. Under the pressure of more than several atmospheres, man, turned self-contained diver, cannot tolerate pure oxygen which, by a mechanism not fully understood, poisons him and may terminate his metabolism.

---

* NOTE: It is assumed that participants in these laboratory exercises are free of upper respiratory tract or lung infections. Under these conditions, 70% alcohol solution is suitable as a sterilizing agent for mouthpieces. If, for example, the determination of the metabolic function of tubercular or emphysematous patients is contemplated, the reader is urged to consult with a medical technologist in order to obtain a more effective germicidal.

Man's need for food and water is met periodically; however, his need for oxygen must be met constantly.

Discussion

The atmosphere consists of nitrogen (79.04%), oxygen (20.93%), and carbon dioxide (0.03%).* Attention is focused on oxygen.

Brain tissue and cardiac tissue cannot tolerate an interrupted supply of oxygen, whereas muscle tissue can tolerate interruptions lasting several minutes. The consequence of these interruptions to the brain and heart ranges from partial to extensive necrosis of these organs; death of the complete organism may result. Blood is the vehicle for oxygen; thus the chemical attraction and delivery of oxygen molecules to trillions of body cells involve the cardiovascular-respiratory system.† Carbon dioxide, a metabolic end-product, is also attracted to and carried by the same vehicle within the same system.

Tissues differ not only in function but also in chemical composition and activity and in rate of heat liberation, heat formation being one of the by-products of biochemical reactions. The direct measurement of the heat liberated by the body serves as an indication of the extent of biochemical activity—the metabolism—taking place within the body. Thus, man can be placed within a chamber of special design (a calorimeter) and the extent of his collective biochemical reactions, reflected by the heat liberated by his body and respiratory gases, can be measured by *direct* means. This technique is aptly labeled *direct calorimetry*.

Heat production resulting from biochemical reactions involves an oxidative process; consequently, the rate of oxygen consumption reflects *indirectly* the rate of metabolic activity. Interpretation of metabolic rate through oxygen consumption values is fittingly called *indirect calorimetry*.

Each of the above calorimetric techniques possesses advantages and disadvantages, but the attractive features of the indirect technique include low capital outlay and versatility. In the succeeding pages, a discussion of direct calorimetry will be omitted.

Indirect calorimetry can be accomplished in either of two divergent ways, viz., by utilizing the closed-circuit system or the open-circuit system.

Closed-circuit indirect calorimetry possesses an appealing simplicity. Essentially, the difference-method is employed: an initial gas volume is noted and after a given time period of subject utilization the final gas

---

* Actually, argon, for example, is present in greater quantity (0.93%) than is carbon dioxide; however, carbon dioxide is of greater interest and importance in the discussion of metabolism. Trace gases such as argon, neon, helium, krypton, xenon, hydrogen, ozone, nitrous oxide, and methane are reflected in the nitrogen percentage.

† Internal as well as external respiration.

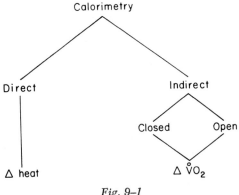

Fig. 9–1

volume is noted. The difference between initial and final volumes indicates the amount consumed. Closed systems must be employed with caution. Using a gasometer, which was designed for the assessment of *basal* metabolism, for exercise energy assessment is inexcusable. Problems stem from ineffective carbon dioxide absorption at high ventilation levels (see Fig. 8–3, text p. 163).*

Open-circuit indirect calorimetry differs from the closed system in that the subject breathes atmospheric air. Attention is directed to the exhaled gases. Exhaled air may be collected either in bags or in gasometers, which facilitate volumetric determination. Essential, however, is an analysis of the composition of the gas. Calculation of oxygen consumption is based upon the nitrogen and oxygen in the sample.

Gas volume varies with temperature and pressure; therefore, for comparisons of volumes to be meaningful the adoption of standard conditions is essential. Standard conditions are effected through the use of the combined laws of Boyle and Charles—through STPD corrections. Oxygen consumption values must be reported at STPD; however, lung volumes will be reported at BTPS.

* Closed-circuit systems may be used in energy cost studies; however, the system requires a high volume pump and an effective carbon dioxide absorber.

Laboratory Exercise Number 20—Calculating Oxygen Consumption $\dot{V}o_2$, Ventilation Equivalent for Oxygen VEo_2, and Reciprocal of VEo_2 by Means of Closed-Circuit Systems

(See text pp. 162–164, 245–250, 252–253, 292)

Required Apparatus and Materials*

Recording spirometer—3-speed kymograph
Barometer, mercury
Nose clip
Mouthpiece, rubber
Oxygen cylinder (300 cu ft), purity: USP
Regulator
Alcohol, 70% solution

Definition of Terms

Oxygen consumption, designated by the symbol $\dot{V}o_2$, is an appropriate descriptive term which signifies the quantification of the oxygen consumed by tissues and organs, or by the body collectively. It is indicative of the rate of metabolism. Other interchangeable terms are "oxygen uptake" and "oxygen intake."

Ventilation equivalent for oxygen, symbolized by VEo_2, denotes the relationship between ventilation and oxygen consumption, hence it serves as an indicator of ventilation efficiency.

The *reciprocal of VEo_2* indicates the rate of oxygen removal per unit ventilation.

Procedure

1. Follow procedural steps 1 through 6 on pages 127–129 and 8 on page 129; however, utilize ventilograph as well (see p. 136).
2. Subject will be seated and will breathe normally; tracings will be of five minutes' duration.
3. Obtain tracings from each subject.

* For approximate cost and for suggested respirometer source, see Appendix B, page 202.

Data Treatment

1. Calculate $\dot{V}o_2$ (see text pp. 245–248); correct to STPD.
2. Calculate minute volume, i.e., ventilation; correct to BTPS.
3. Calculate VEo_2 and reciprocal of VEo_2 (see text pp. 252–253).

Additional Notes

A brief discussion of the definitive term *minute volume,* although repetitious, is necessary. Attention is directed to the *generic* nature of the term. One use of MV may be that of describing *ventilation* per minute of *gas volume.* In this laboratory exercise, ventilation (gas flow) was expressed in terms of volume per minute. Also, oxygen consumption was expressed in cc/minute or ml/minute. Cubic centimeters or millimeters signify *volume* of oxygen *consumed* per *minute.* Thus one can substitute MV for $\dot{V}o_2$. In another section (p. 38) the output of the heart was expressed as a volume of *blood* flow per minute. In that example, MV was used to describe a *liquid* flow or output rate in contrast to using the term to express *gas* flow and *gas* consumption rates.

Minute volume is a *general term* which cannot be reserved solely to describe ventilation. Consequently, substitute formulas for VEo_2 and reciprocal VEo_2 could be expressed as follows:

$$VEo_2 = \frac{MV_L}{MV_{cc}} \times 100$$

$$\text{reciprocal } VEo_2 = \frac{MV_{cc}}{MV_L}$$

For this laboratory exercise, the sitting position was deliberately chosen because it represents a position of comfortable inactivity; however, standing, or lying positions could have been substituted. Any of the above calculations can be made for a multitude of physical expressions, but the open-circuit indirect calorimetry technique must be utilized (see p. 145).

Determination of basal metabolism is usually accomplished with the closed-circuit system. Large volume gasometers (120 L or larger) are usually employed; however, the 9-liter respirometer can be used at $\dot{V}o_2$ rates of the order of 250 cc/minute. Thus, a 30 minute reading can be taken with the 9-liter size. Calculating BMR for each member of the class sounds interesting until the student learns of the conditions that must be met. Subjects must be in a post-absorptive state and rested. Early morning represents the ideal time of day for these conditions to be met; consequently, BMR measurement is not advanced as a laboratory exercise but is suggested as a special project. (Read the discussion *Thermogenesis,* text pp. 166–167.)

Discussion Topics

1. Differentiate between resting metabolic rate and basal metabolic rate.

2. Relate the first law of thermodynamics to metabolism and to energy balance.

3. Outline the steps you would take to ascertain the efficiency of the carbon dioxide absorber.

4. Enumerate the effects of a gas source contaminated by carbon dioxide.

Laboratory Exercise Number 21—Calculating Oxygen Consumption by the Open-Circuit Method

(See text pp. 164–166, 256–260)

Required Apparatus and Materials*

Scholander gas analyzer (see Appendix, pp. 165–172)

Glassware, miscellaneous (see Appendix, p. 165)

Apparatus for open-circuit assessment, bag collection method:

    Dry gas meter with centigrade thermometer

    Nose clip

    Two-way J valve

    4 Stopcocks, T-shape (3-way tap) aluminum

    3 Gas bags, Douglas type, 150 L

    British cloth-covered, corrugated tubing, 24 inch (1 inch ID)

    Smooth rubber tubing, 12-inch (¾ inch ID)

Head band for welder's mask (see Fig. 9–2)

Rack, for Douglas bags (see Fig. 9–2)

Scale, physician's

Electric wall clock with sweep-second hand

Bench, 20.3 cm

Electric metronome (40–208 strokes/min)

Definition of Terms

Review *Definition of Terms,* page 146.

Oxygen debt, a much-used term, reflects the discrepancy between the oxygen requirement of a given task and the actual oxygen consumption during the performance of the task. The debt—the discrepancy—is reflected in the recovery oxygen consumption levels which decrease from high values immediately upon the cessation of the task to levels which become comparable with pre-task levels. The discrepancy is an indication of biochemical, cardiovascular-pulmonary, and biomechanical lag.

Net recovery oxygen, as the term suggests, is a measure of the total or gross recovery oxygen minus the oxygen which would have been consumed (at pre-task rates) had the task not been undertaken.

By calculation, rather than concept, the net recovery oxygen is the oxygen debt.

---

* For approximate cost and for suggested apparatus source, see Appendix B, pages 202–203.

Procedure

1. Read and record barometric pressure (see p. 177).

2. Oil the two gas sample syringe barrels with heavy paraffin oil. With glass marking pencil, label syringes A and B.

3. Zero the micrometer on Scholander analyzer in preparation for first gas sample. (See Appendix p. 168 ff for discussion of Scholander apparatus.)

4. Empty the Douglas bags (see pp. 175–176) and turn stopcock to closed position.

5. Attach mouthpiece to two-way valve, then place in head band, and adjust the head band to subject. Attach nosepiece; also attach hose from valve to stopcock (see Fig. 9–2). Be certain that nose clip is securely fastened and that two-way valve is functioning properly.

6. One student is assigned the task of collecting exhaled air for two consecutive five-minute periods from the subject, who assumes a position of standing rest. Note the valve arrangement in Figure 9–2 which allows for consecutive collection of gas samples.

7. After the first sample has been collected—and during the period in which the second rest sample is being collected—another student will withdraw* a sample of gas for analysis. An additional pair of students will then determine the volume and temperature of the gas in each Douglas bag.† Enter results on data sheet (see Data Sheet 9–1). Repeat procedure for remaining bags.

8. Note from data sheet that, although subject performs work, i.e., five-minute bench-stepping, *only the recovery samples* are collected. During the bench-stepping phase the subject *remains attached* to the bag; however, the stopcock is turned to permit the exhaled air to escape until the work phase is completed. Recovery samples are collected for the intervals indicated: 0–1, 1–3, 3–6, and 6–10 (see Data Sheet 9–1).

9. In addition to the subject, the following personnel are required:
   1 Timer.
   1 Bag transporter—from rack to bag pushers and return.
   2 Bag pushers (see pp. 175–176 and Figs. A–4A and A–4B).
   1 Meter and gas temperature reader.
   2 Spotters—for well-being of subject (see 4, p. 14).
   1 Gas diverter (see Fig. 9–2).
   1 Operator for Scholander analyzer (see pp. 168–172).
   1 Gas-sample collector (see p. 175).

* See syringe withdrawal technique, page 175; see Fig. A–3 also.
† See pages 175–176 and Figs A–4A and A–4B.

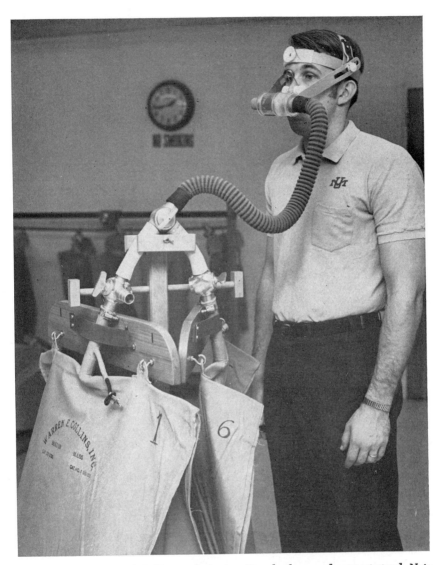

Fig. 9–2.   Open-circuit indirect calorimetry; Douglas bags and support stand. Note position of plug on uppermost stopcock. As indicated by plug position, exhaled gas will flow into bag #1 (pictured with stopcock in open position). Used in this manner, uppermost stopcock serves as a gas diverter. When plug is turned 90 degrees to the right (only direction possible) gas is diverted to other bag. Same type stopcock is secured to Douglas bags; however, when plug is turned 90 degrees to the right, bag is closed off; subject would not experience discomfort because exhaled gas would be vented into atmosphere. Bag numbering eliminates uncertainty of interval sample. Larger portable bag rack is pictured in background.

11

Subject_____ Wt=_____kg

Date_____

P_B _____mmHg

Bench stepping, 5 min @ 20 complete steps/min. Work=_____kgm

	Bag No.	Syringe	Elapsed time min	Vol uncorr L	Gas temp °C	STPD corr	Vol corr L	Time min	MV L	Expired air % O$_2$	CO$_2$	N$_2$
Rest	1	A	0-5									
	2	B	5-10									
	3	C	0-1									
Recovery	1	D	1-3									
	2	A	3-6									
	3	B	6-10									

Data Sheet 9-1

Data Treatment

1. For *each* of the six entries on the data sheet:
   A. Apply STPD correction to gas volumes.
   B. Convert volumes (at STPD) to minute volume.
   C. Calculate $\dot{V}o_2$ from any *one* of the three methods presented in the text:
      (1). By transforming the percentage of each component gas into liters then applying the O_2/N_2 constant (see text p. 257).
      (2). By formula, without nomogram (see text pp. 257–258):

$$\dot{V}o_2 = \frac{MV_{ml}}{100} \times (\%N_2 \text{ exhaled air} \times 0.265 - \%O_2 \text{ exhaled air})$$

   NOTE: Because the product of $\%N_2$ exhaled air $\times$ 0.265 $-$ $\%O_2$ exhaled air yields true $O_2\%$, the formula could be rewritten as:

$$\dot{V}o_2 = \frac{MV_{ml}}{100} \times \text{true } O_2\%$$

      (3). By formula, with nomogram (see text pp. 259–260):

$$\dot{V}o_2 = \frac{\text{True } O_2\%}{100} \times MV$$

   NOTE: Formulas (2) and (3) are merely rearrangements of each other. Formula (2) can be used without the additional requirement of a nomogram; however, the calculation of R requires an additional step whereas (3) requires a nomogram but R can be readily obtained.

2. Calculate the net cost of the recovery phase, in Lo_2 (see text pp. 263–264).

3. Calculate the oxygen debt (see text pp. 264–265).

4. Express $\dot{V}o_2$ in ml/kg/min (see text p. 265). Plot these data graphically.

Additional Notes

The elaborate open-circuit method contrasts sharply with the simplicity of the closed-circuit system. Although simple, the close-circuit method is inadequate (see p. 145).

In this laboratory exercise, many new techniques were introduced. Obviously, the operation can become smoother and the data more reliable as each student becomes proficient at his assigned task. Timers must speak loudly and clearly: "5 seconds before switching . . . 3 seconds . . . 2 seconds . . . SWITCH." Used in this sense, "switch" means to divert gas from one bag into another. Likewise, gas diverters must be certain that the exhaled air is being directed into the proper bag and, equally as important, that the stopcock valve on the previously collected sample is closed. Gas analysts must strive for speed with accuracy—a sign of proficiency. With practice, double determinations can be accomplished within 12 minutes. Bag pushers should strive to exert constant pressure on the bags.

An inexpensive method of emptying the bags involves the use of a household vacuum cleaner motor which *pulls* the collected sample through the gas meter. Flow rates can be reduced by using pinch

Fig. 9–3.   Motor blower with rheostat control used as a pull-pump for bag-emptying purposes. Flow rate can be adjusted by varying rheostat. This versatile motor is also used in the closed-circuit, helium equilibration technique for residual volume estimation. Also pictured is a pressure control which automatically switches off motor when the Douglas bag is empty. A vacuum cleaner will perform a similar function.

clamps on the rubber tubing which connects meter outlet to vacuum motor. Another technique involves the use of a Variac control, wired to the motor, which serves to reduce the motor revolutions and hence reduces the rate of gas flow. All tubing connections must be secure in

Fig. 9–4. The gasometer used in an open-circuit system. Note that carbon dioxide container has been removed. Gas samples for analysis are taken from top of bell. A mixing motor (atop bell) prevents stratification of gases. Note the meter stick and kymograph drum. Uncorrected volume can be easily ascertained by using a measuring stick calibrated in volumes based on bell factor (cc/mm) × displacement (mm).

order to eliminate air leaks which will inflate the volume reading.

Gasometers of large volume—120 L or larger—can be used in an open-circuit system. Essentially, the gasometer serves as a huge collecting chamber, thus replacing the collapsible collecting bags. It also provides a measure of the volume and temperature of the exhaled gas thus replacing the gas meter—and bag pushers—as well.

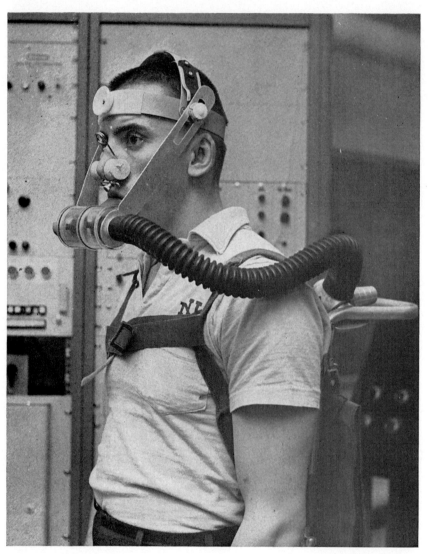

Fig. 9–5.   A portable rack for measurement of energy cost. Note adjustable head harness. The energy cost of wearing the rack, bag, and other apparatus was calculated to be statistically nonsignificant.

Because of its capacity, a gasometer is most conveniently suited to the task of estimating basal metabolism by means of the open-circuit technique. Its large volume affords the opportunity to calculate mean values of successive, lengthy intervals, thus providing an accurate estimation. Gasometers are not limited to estimations of BMR. They may be used to collect any exhaled sample; however, if consecutive intervals are desired an additional gasometer is needed. Obviously, they lack portability. Finally, gasometers represent an added expense and this term is inconsonant with the message of this text.

If available, gasometers may generate an additional laboratory exercise: an estimation of resting metabolic rates utilizing collapsible bags in comparison with the gasometer.

The final note relates to mode of calculating oxygen consumption. Perhaps the student should consider becoming a systematist. Additional columns on the data sheet (see Data Sheet 9–1) can be labeled and the rewards of said effort exhibited in *reduced* calculation time. As an example, if the nomogram is used, an additional column on the data sheet could be labeled "True O_2%." The student could then enter the true O_2% values for each entry. If *necessary* an adjacent column might be labeled True O_2%/100 and would reflect the manipulation of the decimal point two places to the left. Lastly, multiplication of MV by True O_2% would complete the calculation.

A similar system could be employed for each of the other calculation methods.

Discussion Topics

1. What is the significance of expressing oxygen consumption as a function of body weight?

2. What problems can be encountered in oxygen debt assessment?

3. How would you proceed to calculate V_T from the open-circuit technique? Enumerate the steps.

4. Were cardiac frequency monitored, what relationship would you expect it to have to oxygen consumption? Explain.

Laboratory Exercise Number 22—Step-Test: A Physiological Appraisal

(Read text pp. 263–264, 267–269, 287–289)

Required Apparatus and Materials

The same apparatus as that required for Laboratory Exercise Number 21 with the following additions:
Stethoscope
1 Additional Douglas bag, 150 L, fitted with sampling tubing and stopcock (see pp. 173–174)
Bench, 40.6 cm

Definition of Terms

Read *Definition of Terms,* pages 146 and 149.

Physiological appraisal, in the sense of the present laboratory exercise, conveys a multivariate approach to step-test performance.

Gross and net cost of exercise may be expressed as a quantity of oxygen consumed or as the amount of kilocalories expended not only in the performance of the exercise but also in the recovery from the performance as well. As implied, *gross cost* is an *all inclusive* term, i.e., consideration is given to the total quantity of oxygen or total number of kilocalories expended. *Net cost* represents a refinement in calculation in that the resting rate is deducted from the total expenditure.

Generally, efficiency is expressed as a ratio of output to input. When applied to the performing human being, *efficiency* is expressed as a ratio of accomplishment to energy requirement of the task. In comparison with *gross efficiency, net efficiency* represents a refined expression in the sense that the resting metabolic rate is arithmetically removed, hence the expression yields greater meaning. As with any ratio which is reported as a percentage, numerator and denominator must be expressed in the same units. Work is commonly expressed as kilogram-meters whereas the energy requirement of the task, the denominator, is commonly expressed as volume of oxygen consumed. Consequently, the volume of consumed oxygen must be converted into kilogram-meter equivalent units. Conversion of numerator and denominator into other equivalent units is possible (see text pp. 287–289).

Caloric cost or *energy cost* is a reflection of the oxygen consumed in the performance of the task and in the recovery from the task and represents a term which is in common use. Generally, the relationship $1 \text{ L } O_2$

= 5 kcal is used to express the caloric expenditure of human perform-ance. This relationship is dependent upon the value of the respiratory exchange ratio.

Respiratory exchange ratio, symbolized by R, is representative of the relationship between the quantity of carbon dioxide produced to the oxygen consumed during any phase of metabolic activity.

Cardiac output, or *minute volume* of the heart, is an indication of the volume of blood ejected per minute by both ventricles.

Cardiac index is an expression of the minute volume of the heart rela-tive to such physical characteristics as height and weight represented by body surface area.

The extent of tissue oxygen delivery per pulse beat per minute is called the *oxygen pulse.*

Procedure

1. Make ready the Scholander apparatus, page 165 ff; syringes, page 169; and Douglas bags, page 173 ff.

2. Record the barometric pressure and the subject's weight on the data sheet (Data Sheet 9–2).

3. Select one of the duties to be performed (see p. 150). Two addi-tional duties are included. One duty is that of counting the respiration frequency per minute by observing the opening or closing of the rubber inlet disc within the valve during the following intervals: rest 6–7, work 2–3, 4–5, recovery 0–1, 2–3, 9–10, and 14–15.

The other duty entails the counting of cardiac frequency for the rest and recovery intervals listed above. Locate the stethoscope head over the left third intercostal space at the mid-clavicular line.

4. Outfit the subject (see step 5, p. 150).

5. Set metronome at 100

6. Collect, meter, and analyze the exhaled gas samples for the inter-vals indicated on the data sheet (Data Sheet 9–2). Note bag sequence. A pause of few minutes' duration between the end of rest and beginning of work is permissible; however, the interval from the beginning of work to the cessation of recovery—20 minutes—*must be continuous.*

Data Treatment

1. Calculate the following:
    A. Gross and net cost of exercise (see text p. 263).
    B. Gross and net efficiency (see text p. 264).
    C. Energy cost of step-testing (see text p. 264).
    D. R for rest 6–7; work 3–4, 4–5; and recovery 0–1, 5–6, 14–15 (see p. 153).

Subject_____ Wt=_____ kg

Date_____

P_B _____ mmHg

Bag No.	Syringe	Elapsed time mins	Vol uncorr L	Gas temp °C	STPD corr	Vol corr L	Time min	MV L	Expired air % O_2	CO_2	N_2
Rest (sitting) 1	A	0-7									
Work ___kgm 1	A	0-1									
2	B	1-3									
3	C	3-5									
4	D	0-1									
Recovery (sitting) 1	A	1-3									
2	B	3-6									
3	C	6-10									
4	D	10-15									

Data Sheet 9-2

    E. Cardiac output and stroke volume for rest 6–7 and recovery
       0–1, 2–3, 9–10, 14–15 (see text pp. 267–268).
    F. Cardiac index and oxygen pulse for rest and recovery 0–1, 14–15
       (see text pp. 268–269).
  2. Plot the results graphically: $\dot{V}o_2$ ml/kg/min as a function of time.

Additional Notes

Unless the Scholander operator is expert, he may lose his composure
thus risking faulty analysis. To reduce this possibility, several additional
gas sampling syringes are advocated.

The barrels of all syringes must be clearly coded to correspond with
particular samples. Provided the syringes are properly oiled and the
needles properly thrust into rubber stoppers, sample analysis can proceed
with deliberation.

Note, from Data Sheet 9–2, the coding of syringes to correspond with
particular intervals. (Obviously the use of nine Douglas bags and nine
sampling syringes—one for each entry—represents one manner of solving
the problem; however, other organizational practices can be effectively
utilized. One practice is outlined below.)

With the availability of four sampling syringes and four Douglas bags,
a pause between the termination of the rest interval and the beginning
of work is suggested. Once the gas sample has been withdrawn from
bags 1 through 4 (representing work and first minute recovery intervals),
the gas must be metered at a gingerly pace in order that the bags become readied for use during the remainder of the recovery phase. The
source of tension is now lessened because the recovery gases can remain
in the bags until the syringes become available.

Many bag-sampling syringe arrangements are possible; however, the
suggested simple arrangement leaves little room for confusion and error.
One final arrangement involving two Douglas bags (1, 2) and six sampling syringes is suggested; however, bag evacuation must be accomplished
by pump rather than bag pushers:

	Bag No.	Syringe	Interval
Rest	1	A	0– 7
	(pause for analysis of rest sample)		
Work	1	A	0– 1
	2	B	1– 3
	1	C	3– 5
Recovery	2	D	0– 1
	1	E	1– 3
	2	F	3– 6
	1	A	6–10
	2	B	10–15

With the above arrangement the Scholander operator need not hurry the analysis of work samples in syringes A and B because the last two recovery samples can be left in bags 1 and 2 until the syringes become available.

The appraisal, suggested in the title of this laboratory exercise, could have become more complete. To exemplify, elgons could have been utilized, shell and core temperatures measured, and blood and urine analyzed. The student was spared the effort.

The reader will note that the calculation of kilogram meters of work involves only the positive phase. Assessment of the negative phase can be accomplished; however, the results are likely to be reported in terms of energy expenditure for both positive and negative phases.

Discussion Topics

1. Enumerate the strengths and weaknesses of R as an indicator of the severity of physical performance.

2. Metabolically, how would you classify the step-test used in this laboratory exercise? Document your answer.

3. What is the rationale of expressing $\dot{V}o_2$ in ml/kg/minute?

4. Discuss the effect of pure oxygen administration on recovery. Document your reply.

Concluding Remarks

An apparatus and equipment inventory must be geared to course enrollment. Keen administrators fully understand the necessity of small-group instruction in which everyone participates.

Not to be overlooked is the opportunity to hold down laboratory costs by purchasing reagents, glassware, and supplies through a large purchaser as the department of chemistry. Also, if an analytical balance is to be given occasional use, e.g., only when preparing solutions for the Scholander apparatus, then this operation can be conducted in the chemistry laboratory.

The quest for apparatus and equipment can be intense. Outside of the usual channels of purchase, state surplus property agencies* must be contacted and depots visited. Surplus Douglas bags would constitute a rare find; however, three-way tap stopcocks are occasionally found. Large gasometers in need of some repair and calibration have been located at these sites. Treadmills have been obtained through this channel. Older model paramagnetic, oxygen analyzers are frequently acquired through this source. A variety of electric motors is usually assured as are plentiful supplies of wire, electronic components, and microswitches.

Electronic apparatus seemingly always assures convenience. In many instances, repeat accuracy and absolute accuracy are immensely improved; however, accuracy is not to be always associated with price and gadgetry. While it cannot offer convenience of assay or of continuous monitoring, the low-priced Scholander analyzer possesses the potential for accuracy which is comparable to that of the most expensive electronic (gas) analyzers.

Substitute items can often be used. To exemplify, plastic bags may be used in place of the durable, canvas-covered, rubber Douglas bags. These plastic bags are less expensive and less durable. For the interested reader, the articles of Perkins[3] and of Johnson and colleagues[2] are suggested.

Most important to the bag user is the consideration of carbon dioxide loss. Gas storage of short duration, i.e., less than one-half hour, presents no problem; however, diffusion of carbon dioxide is markedly noticeable beyond the sixth hour. For additional information relative to carbon dioxide loss, see Shepard[4] and Balchum and associates.[1]

---

* Apparatus, equipment, and components typically filter down from the various branches of the Armed Forces (as "excess items") through the Department of Defense and General Services Administration which releases the items to the states as "donable property."

REFERENCES

1. Balchum, O. J., Hartman, S. A., Slonim, N. B., Dressler, S. H., and Ravin, A.: The permeability of the Douglas-type bag to respiratory gases. *J. Lab. Clin. Med.*, *41*:268–280, 1953.

2. Johnson, R. E., Robbins, F., Schilke, R., Molé, P., Harris, J., and Wakat, D.: A versatile system for measuring oxygen consumption in man. *J. Appl. Physiol.*, *22*:377–379, 1967.

3. Perkins, J. F.: Plastic Douglas bags. *J. Appl. Physiol.*, *6*:445–447, 1954.

4. Shepard, R. J.: A critical examination of the Douglas bag technique. *J. Physiol.*, *127*:515–524, 1955.

APPENDIX A

SCHOLANDER APPARATUS
(Reagents, Glassware, Miscellaneous, Operation)

1. Reagents and other equipment:
   A. Reagents*:

Sulfuric acid, sp gr 1.84, 16 oz	$ 1.50
Sodium hydrosulfite $Na_2S_2O_4$, 16 oz	1.85
2-Anthraquinonesulfonic acid, sodium salt, 100 gm	3.50
Glycerol, neutral, 1 lb	0.95
Potassium dichromate $K_2Cr_2O_7$, 4 oz	1.25
Potassium hydroxide KOH, 16 oz	0.85
Mercury suitable for microanalysis, 1 lb	19.50
Piccolite X† (Piccolyte, dry resin), 1 lb	1.05
Toluene (or xylol), 1 pt	0.85
Stopcock grease, 25-gm tube	0.75
Paraffin oil, heavy USP 1X, 1 pt	0.85

   B. Glassware:

Glass tuberculin syringe, 1 cc	3.00
Glass syringe, glass tip, 5 cc	2.70
4 Glass syringes, glass tip, 10 cc, @ 3.60 each	14.40
1 Glass syringe, glass tip, 30 cc	4.00
6 Evacuated tubes, "Vacutainers"	0.60
Beaker, 50 ml, graduated	0.75
Beaker, 500 ml, graduated	0.75
Mortar and pestle, glass, 8 oz	4.25
Erlenmeyer flask, 25 ml, with stopper	0.60
6 Needles, #24, short gauge, ¾ inch, @ 0.50 each	3.00
12 Needles, assorted, @ 0.50 each (see Van Liew[2] for combinations)	6.00

* Suggested source: Arthur H. Thomas Co., Vine Street at Third, P.O. Box 779, Philadelphia, Pennsylvania 19105.

† Source: General Biological Inc., 8200 South Hoyne Avenue, Chicago, Illinois 60620.

C. Miscellaneous apparatus for Scholander use:

Filter pump aspirator (brass)	2.75
Rubber tubing, pure gum, ¼ inch bore, 10-foot carton	3.80
Filter paper	
6 Rubber stoppers size 00	0.60
Balance, analytical	500.00

2. Assemble the Scholander apparatus, following instructions given in Scholander's paper.[1]

Fill the following with mercury: the micrometer chamber, micrometer burette, bottom portion of reaction chamber unit, and leveling bulb to level indicated in Figure A–1. Fill tube K with acid rinsing solution. Fill water bath to level of narrowest upper portion of thermobarometer (if filled to level indicated the apparatus could not be tilted without spilling water).

3. Preparation instructions for the solutions given in the following paragraphs are the same as those given by Scholander[1] except for the material enclosed in brackets, which represents my departure from Scholander's procedure:

Acid Rinsing Solution. Into a large beaker or Erlenmeyer flask, pour 400 cc of distilled water from a measuring cylinder. With a 1-cc tuberculin syringe without a needle, add 1 cc of H_2SO_4 (sp gr 1.84). To this add 72 g of anhydrous Na_2SO_4 a little at a time while continuously agitating the container to dissolve the salt. Without agitation the salt will cake and require hours to dissolve; with agitation the salt dissolves in a few minutes.

To bring the vapor tension of the acid down to that of the absorbents, glycerol is added to the solution. Pour a little more than 21 cc of glycerol into a syringe, insert the plunger, expel the air from the syringe, and adjust the amount of glycerol to 21 cc and then add it to the solution through the nozzle of the syringe. Fifty cc of the solution are stored in the centrifuge tube immersed in the water bath of the gas analysis apparatus. So that the analysis is not vitiated, approximately 40 mg of pulverized potassium dichromate are added to the tube to destroy any trace of hydrosulfite which might be present. Dichromate is also used in the carbon dioxide absorbent for the same purpose.

Carbon Dioxide Absorber. In a wide-mouthed vessel, mix the following: 100 cc of water, 11 g of KOH, and 40 mg of potassium dichromate. Fill a 2- or 5-cc syringe fitted with a short-gauge, No. 24 needle with the solution.

Oxygen Absorber. SOLUTION A. Place 6 g of KOH in 100 cc of water. After mixing, store in a wide-mouthed vessel.

POWDER A. Mix thoroughly in a mortar 0.1 g of sodium anthraquinone-

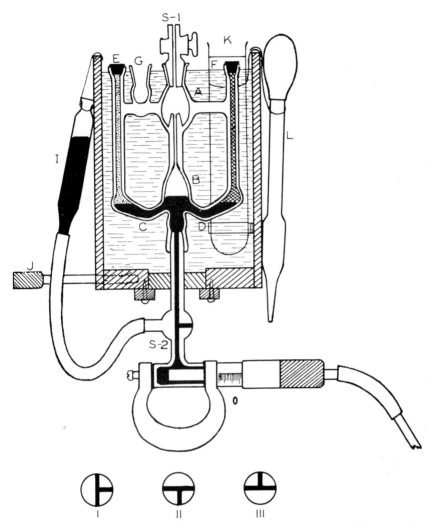

Fig. A–1.   Analyzer for accurate estimation of respiratory gases in 0.5-cc samples.
A, Compensating chamber (thermobarometer); B, reaction chamber; C, side arm for
carbon dioxide absorber; D, side arm for oxygen absorber; E and F, solid vaccine
bottle stoppers; G, receptacle for stopcock S-1; S-2, micrometer burette; O, micrometer; I, leveling bulb; J, handle for tilting of apparatus; K, tube for storing acid rinsing solution; L, pipette for rinsing acid. [Transfer of gas sample to the analyzer is
accomplished by the Van Liew technique, modified; see p. 169.] (From Scholander.[1]
Courtesy of American Society of Biological Chemists, Inc.)

12

beta-sulfonate with 20 g of fresh sodium hydrosulfite ($Na_2S_2O_4$) and store in a stoppered vessel.

SOLUTION B. [In a Vacutainer,* place 0.6 g of Powder A; replace stopper. Evacuate the atmospheric gas trapped within the tube by means of the aspirating technique. Empty a 10-cc, oiled syringe† by pushing the plunger into the barrel. Insert the hypodermic needle (attached to the syringe) through the stopper of the Vacutainer and withdraw the plunger slowly. Then, remove and empty the syringe, and repeat the procedure. Draw approximately 5.5 cc of Solution A into a 10-cc syringe fitted with a No. 24 hypodermic needle. Invert the syringe and expel all the air and all but 5 cc of the solution and then inject the solution into the evacuated tube containing 0.6 g of Powder A.‡ Dissolve the powder by holding the lower end of the Vacutainer under hot water flowing from a faucet; shake the Vacutainer gently. When the characteristic ruby color appears and Powder A has been fully dissolved, cool the contents (now called Solution B) of the Vacutainer to room temperature by immersing the tube end in a stream of cold water.] With the least possible air contact, draw the lower three-fourths of Solution B into a 5-cc syringe fitted with a short-gauge, No. 24 needle. Equilibrate with nitrogen at atmospheric pressure by leaving a small bubble in the syringe. [Introduce the tip of the needle into a size 00 rubber stopper. This reduces considerably the risk of saturating the oxygen absorber with the 21% oxygen present in the atmosphere.]

4. Aspirate chamber C by using an empty syringe fitted with a short-gauge, No. 24 hypodermic needle. Introduce the carbon dioxide absorber through rubber stopper E (Fig. A–1)—into *left* side of reaction chamber unit. Aspirate chamber D; then introduce the oxygen absorber through stopper F—into *right* side. Aspirate all air bubbles from chambers C and D. *Keep chambers filled to level indicated in Figure A–1.*

NOTE: Chambers will not require further aspiration unless the apparatus is partially dismantled, i.e., reaction chamber unit removed to permit washing of the water bath.

5. Preparing the analyzer for the introduction of the gas sample:
    A. Place stopcock S 1 in receptacle G.
    B. Turn S 2 to position I and return micrometer setting to zero. Carefully watch the rise of the mercury in reaction chamber B.

---

* Vacutainers are blood-collecting tubes for venipuncture sampling; specify tubes without anticoagulant.

† Utilize one of the syringes used to withdraw gas samples for analysis.

‡ Because almost 21% oxygen is present in the atmosphere, great care must be exercised in the preparation of the oxygen absorber. Neither Powder A nor Solution A, considered separately, can become saturated. By introducing Solution A into Powder A, in the manner previously described, the dissolution process takes place in an anaerobic medium. The carbon dioxide absorbent presents little problem because of the small amount present in the atmosphere (0.03%).

The mercury column, with micrometer setting at zero, should *fill* chamber B. If micrometer cannot be zeroed because of impending mercury spillage into thermobarometer A, turn S 2 to position II and proceed to zero the micrometer. Return S 2 to position I. With pipette L, half-fill thermobarometer A with acid rinsing solution.

6. Before introducing and analyzing the gas sample, as described below read *Technique of Withdrawing Gas Sample with Syringe from Douglas Bag* (p. 175 and Fig. A–3).

    A. Remove rubber stopper from needle tip of sampling syringe and hold syringe in *semi-vertical position** (See Fig. A–2). Slip adaptor† over sampling needle and introduce into compensating chamber (A). Seat the adaptor firmly in place. NOTE: Owing

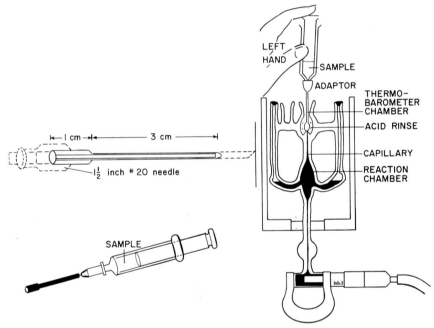

Fig. A–2.   An adaptor close-up shown at left, which is slipped over the needle, makes possible the direct transfer of gas from sampling syringe to Scholander analyzer. Van Liew[2] states: "An adaptor for use with no. 24 hypodermic needles can be made from a no. 20 needle. The point and part of the butt are cut off and the shoulder is turned down on a lathe. The no. 24/no. 20 combination of sampling needle and adaptor is convenient, but other combinations can be used—for example, 20/17, 21/18, 22/18, 23/19, 25/20, 25/21, 26/21, and 28/22." (Redrawn from Van Liew.[2] Courtesy of American Physiological Society.)

   * The semi-vertical position represents a modification of the Van Liew[2] transfer technique. The pressure on the sample gas created by the position of the plunger is sufficient to prevent contamination of the sample gas with ambient air.

   † Combinations of sampling needles and adaptors are presented by Van Liew.[2]

to the force exerted by the vertical position of the plunger, some of the gas sample will escape as evidenced by the gas bubbles in the rinse solution which half fills the chamber.

B. With S 2 already in position I (see 5B above), screw the micrometer *slowly out*—counterclockwise—until the gas meniscus reaches the index on the capillary tube. Watch carefully (the colorless gas in combination with the transparent quality of water and glassware requires close observation of the meniscus). Turn S 2 to position II and zero the micrometer by adjusting it to 0.5 *past* zero. Then, turn S 2 back to position I and screw the micrometer out until an approximate micrometer setting of 18 is attained (or less if sample is small). Remove the sampling syringe and adaptor (and replace rubber stopper on needle tip*. Screw micrometer out—slowly—until the rinsing solution is sucked into the reaction chamber *to the level of the index* on the capillary tube. Record the micrometer setting; this is V_1. Insert stopcock S 1 into compensating chamber and close tap.

C. Introduce a small amount of the carbon dioxide absorber into the reaction chamber by tilting the water bath gently to the LEFT. Switch the motor ON. Screw *in* the micrometer to compensate for the decrease in gas sample volume resulting from carbon dioxide absorption. Keep the gas meniscus at the level of the index. When the gas meniscus remains stationary at the index, switch motor off and record micrometer setting as V_2.

D. Introduce a small amount of the oxygen absorber by tilting the water bath gently to the RIGHT. (The mercury in chamber D should be covered with a 1-mm layer of absorbent.) Switch the motor ON. Once again, screw *in* the micrometer to keep the gas meniscus at the level of the index. NOTE: Because the decrease in gas sample volume will be rapid—resulting from fast absorption of oxygen—the micrometer will require constant adjustment in order to keep the gas meniscus at the level of the index. To lose track of the meniscus is to risk the loss of an analysis. When the meniscus remains at the index, switch the motor off and record the micrometer setting as V_3.

E. Open stopcock S 1 and remove it to receptacle G. Screw *in* the micrometer until the meniscus of the absorbing solution reaches the index. The micrometer setting *should* be at zero ± 0.5 mm.

F. Turn S 2 to position III and aspirate the spent absorbing solution. NOTE: In position III, the leveling bulb I is connected with the reaction chamber B; consequently the leveling bulb must

---

* This practice permits an additional analysis. Double determinations are especially desirable when conducting research.

be manipulated to prevent the mercury from spilling into compensating chamber A and becoming subsequently lost in the process of aspiration. Manipulating the leveling bulb requires practice (the dense mercury *responds quickly* to changes in reservoir L). (It might be well for the beginner to grasp the bulb with the left thumb and index and middle fingers and to raise or lower the bulb while maintaining contact between the extended fourth finger and the outer portion of the water bath.) When mercury column fills chamber B, hold leveling bulb steady while turning S 2 to position II

G. Fill compensating chamber to neck level with acid rinsing solution. Grasp leveling bulb, turn S 2 to position III, and manipulate bulb so as to suck the rinsing solution into reaction chamber B to a level just below the side arm openings to chambers C and D. Move the acid rinsing solution about by alternately raising and lowering the leveling bulb several times. Return acid rinsing solution to chamber A, aspirate, replace with fresh acid rinsing solution, and repeat the rinsing process. Aspirate.

H. Half-fill chamber A with acid rinsing solution; turn S 2 to position I. Analysis has been completed, reaction chamber rinsed, and analyzer is once again ready for another gas sample. Start again with 5 above.

7. Calculations: Answers are expressed in cc/100 cc original sample, dry.

$$CO_2 \text{ cc/100 cc dry} = \frac{V_1 - V_2}{V_1} \times 100$$

$$O_2 \text{ cc/100 cc dry} = \frac{V_2 - V_3}{V_1} \times 100$$

$$N_2 \text{ cc/100 cc, dry} = \frac{V_3}{V_1} \times 100$$

Results are considered to be satisfactory when duplicates for carbon dioxide, oxygen, and nitrogen agree within 0.03%.

Example:

$$V_1 = 19.855, \quad V_2 = 19.385, \quad V_3 = 15.793$$

$$CO_2 = \frac{19.855 - 19.385}{19.855} = \frac{.470}{19.855} = 2.37\%$$

$$O_2 = \frac{19.385 - 15.793}{19.855} = \frac{3.592}{19.855} = 18.09\%$$

$$N_2 = \frac{15.793}{19.855} = 79.54\%$$

REFERENCES

1. Scholander, P. F.: Analyzer for accurate estimation of respiratory gases in one-half cubic centimeter samples. *J. Biol. Chem., 167*:235–250, 1947.

2. Van Liew, H. D.: Transfer and storage of small volumes of gas for the Scholander analyzer. *J. Appl. Physiol., 16*:578–580, 1961.

THE DOUGLAS BAG

Readying the Douglas Bag

Required Apparatus and Materials	Approximate Cost
Douglas bag, 150-Liter	$110.00
Rubber tubing,* thin-wall, ¼-inch bore × 2 feet, @ 50¢ ft.	1.00
Glass tubing, 7 mm O.D., 1.0 mm wall, 4 foot length	0.25
Hofmann clamp, open jaw, ½ inch	0.60
Tubing clamp (aero-seal, self-locking, worm-gear type) size 24	0.40

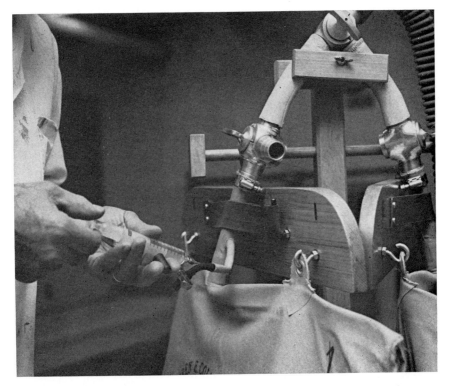

Fig. A–3. Withdrawing gas sample from Douglas bag. Note rubber stop (between fingers) which is used to cap needle. Sample can also be withdrawn from sampling tap of stopcock.

* Rubber and glass tubing are of sufficient quantity for six bags.

Procedure

1. Attach a length of black rubber tubing (approx. 8 cm) to the side outlet tube of the Douglas bag. This is accomplished by inserting a short piece of sturdy plastic or glass tubing (approx. 5 cm) halfway *into* the side outlet tubing. Rubber tubing is slipped over the glass tubing and butts the side outlet tube. Overlap joint with electrical tape. Fold-over and shut off end of rubber tubing with Hofmann clamp.

2. Attach a three-way tap stopcock to the flexible rubber connecting tube. Secure with self-locking worm-gear clamp. Be certain that aluminum stopcock is properly placed; allowance must be made for air flow into the bag and with a one-quarter turn of the plug the contents of the bag must be sealed off.

3. Attach to hanging board and rack (see Figs. 9–2 and A–3).

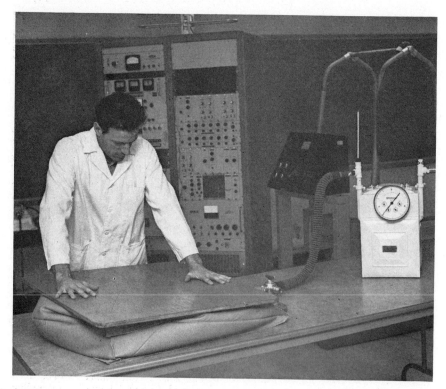

Fig. A–4A.   Emptying the Douglas bag. Steady pressure applied to bag results in constant flow rate which contributes to accuracy. Meter must be zeroed before valve is opened. Note thermometer at meter inlet.

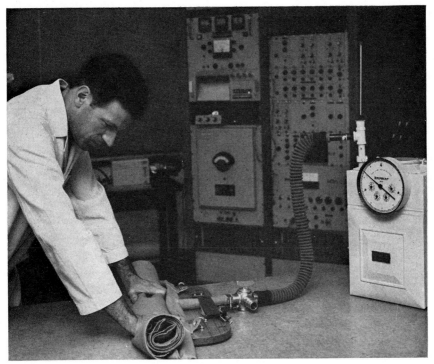

Fig. A–4B.   Final step in emptying the Douglas bag. NOTE: Bag pushing and roll-ing contribute to rubber breakdown, and fabric tear, and eventual leaks. The use of a vacuum motor is preferred to the bag-pushing technique because (1) bag life is prolonged and, more importantly, (2) constant flow rates, which are essential to accuracy, are achieved. (See Fig. 9–3.)

Technique of Withdrawing Gas Sample with Syringe from Douglas Bag

1. Gas sample may be withdrawn from rubber tubing attached to side outlet of Douglas bag or from the sampling tap on newer model stopcocks.

2. Insert the needle of an empty 10-cc syringe into the rubber tubing and fill the syringe by drawing the plunger. *With needle still inserted,* empty the syringe. After repeating this procedure several times, fill the syringe, withdraw the needle, and cap the needle immediately by thrust-ing it into a size 00 rubber stopper.

Emptying the Douglas Bag

1. Lay the Douglas bag on a flat, smooth surface adjacent to the gas meter and connect bag to meter. Be certain that the *meter is zeroed.*

2. Lay a flat, smooth piece of plywood on top of the bag, open the stopcock, and apply steady pressure to the board.

3. When the gas flow ceases, *close the stopcock,** remove board, then continue by rolling up the bag from the bottom and simultaneously *opening* the stopcock. Continue until bag is tightly rolled and, *while maintaining the tight roll,* close the stopcock. Return the bag to the hangar.

* By this technique, air is prevented from being drawn back into the bag from the meter.

READING THE BAROMETER

1. Adjust the peg in the mercury pool until the tip of the peg is in *contact* with the mercury. This establishes the zero point of the scale.

2. Slide the vernier plate (located between the scales) until the *bottom edge is aligned with the top of the mercury column.*

3. Read the barometric pressure (P_B) in metric units. NOTE: The scale is usually graduated in centimeter units, therefore, the reading must be converted to millimeters. The *fraction,* established by the *alignment* of graduations on adjacent scales, is read in 0.1-mm units from the *vernier* scale. (See Fig. A–5.)

4. Make the necessary temperature corrections (mercury expands as temperature increases, vice versa) (see Table A–1).

Fig. A–5. Detail of vernier plate on barometer. Note alignment of 0.7 mm on vernier with adjacent line on cm scale. Observed P_B in this example is 741.7 mm Hg. Temperature correction is also necessary (see step 4 and Table A–1).

Table A–1. Temperature Corrections for Mercury, Barometer Readings

Observed Height (mm)

Temp. °C	640	650	660	670	680	690	700	710	720	730	740	750	760	770
10	1.09	1.11	1.13	1.14	1.16	1.18	1.19	1.21	1.23	1.25	1.26	1.28	1.30	1.31
11	1.20	1.22	1.24	1.26	1.28	1.29	1.31	1.33	1.35	1.37	1.39	1.41	1.43	1.45
12	1.31	1.33	1.35	1.37	1.39	1.41	1.43	1.45	1.47	1.49	1.51	1.54	1.56	1.58
13	1.42	1.44	1.46	1.49	1.51	1.53	1.55	1.57	1.60	1.62	1.64	1.66	1.69	1.71
14	1.53	1.55	1.57	1.60	1.62	1.65	1.67	1.69	1.72	1.74	1.77	1.79	1.81	1.84
15	1.64	1.66	1.69	1.71	1.74	1.76	1.79	1.82	1.84	1.87	1.89	1.92	1.94	1.97
16	1.75	1.77	1.80	1.83	1.85	1.88	1.91	1.94	1.96	1.99	2.02	2.05	2.07	2.10
17	1.85	1.88	1.91	1.94	1.97	2.00	2.03	2.06	2.09	2.12	2.14	2.17	2.20	2.23
18	1.96	1.99	2.02	2.05	2.08	2.12	2.15	2.18	2.21	2.24	2.27	2.30	2.33	2.36
19	2.07	2.10	2.14	2.17	2.20	2.23	2.27	2.30	2.33	2.36	2.40	2.43	2.46	2.49
20	2.18	2.21	2.25	2.28	2.32	2.35	2.38	2.42	2.45	2.49	2.52	2.56	2.59	2.62
21	2.29	2.32	2.36	2.40	2.43	2.47	2.50	2.54	2.58	2.61	2.65	2.68	2.72	2.75
22	2.40	2.43	2.47	2.51	2.55	2.58	2.62	2.66	2.70	2.73	2.77	2.81	2.85	2.88
23	2.51	2.54	2.58	2.62	2.66	2.70	2.74	2.78	2.82	2.86	2.90	2.94	2.98	3.02
24	2.61	2.65	2.70	2.74	2.78	2.82	2.86	2.90	2.94	2.98	3.02	3.06	3.10	3.15
25	2.72	2.77	2.81	2.85	2.89	2.94	2.98	3.02	3.06	3.11	3.15	3.19	3.23	3.28
26	2.83	2.87	2.92	2.96	3.01	3.05	3.10	3.14	3.19	3.23	3.27	3.32	3.36	3.41
27	2.94	2.99	3.03	3.08	3.12	3.17	3.22	3.26	3.31	3.35	3.40	3.45	3.49	3.54
28	3.05	3.10	3.14	3.19	3.24	3.29	3.33	3.38	3.43	3.48	3.52	3.57	3.62	3.67
29	3.16	3.21	3.25	3.30	3.35	3.40	3.45	3.50	3.55	3.60	3.65	3.70	3.75	3.80

30	3.26	3.32	3.37	3.42	3.47	3.52	3.57	3.62	3.67	3.72	3.77	3.83	3.88	3.93
31	3.37	**3.42**	3.48	3.53	3.58	3.64	3.69	3.74	3.79	3.85	3.90	3.95	4.00	4.06
32	3.48	**3.53**	3.59	3.64	3.70	**3.75**	**3.81**	3.86	**3.92**	**3.97**	4.02	**4.08**	4.13	4.19
33	3.59	3.64	3.70	3.76	3.81	3.87	3.92	3.98	4.04	4.09	4.15	4.21	4.26	4.32
34	3.70	3.75	3.81	3.87	3.93	3.99	4.04	4.10	4.16	4.22	4.27	4.33	4.39	4.45
35	3.80	3.86	3.92	3.98	4.04	4.10	4.16	4.22	4.28	4.34	4.40	4.46	4.52	4.58
36	3.91	3.97	4.04	4.10	4.16	4.22	4.28	4.34	4.40	4.46	4.52	4.59	4.65	4.71
37	4.02	4.08	4.15	4.21	4.27	4.33	4.40	4.46	4.52	4.59	4.65	4.71	4.77	4.84
38	4.13	4.19	4.26	4.32	4.39	4.45	4.52	4.58	4.65	4.71	4.77	4.84	4.90	4.97
39	4.24	4.30	4.37	4.44	4.50	4.57	4.63	4.70	4.77	4.83	4.90	4.97	5.03	5.10
40	4.34	4.41	4.48	4.55	4.62	4.68	4.75	4.82	4.89	4.96	5.02	5.09	5.16	5.23
41	4.45	4.52	4.59	4.66	4.73	4.80	4.87	4.94	5.01	5.08	5.15	5.22	5.29	5.36
42	4.56	4.63	4.70	4.77	4.85	4.92	4.99	5.06	5.13	5.20	5.27	5.34	5.42	5.49
43	4.67	4.74	4.81	4.89	4.96	5.03	5.11	5.18	5.25	5.32	5.40	5.47	5.54	5.62
44	4.78	4.85	4.92	5.00	5.07	5.15	5.22	5.30	5.37	5.45	5.52	5.60	5.67	5.75
45	4.88	4.96	5.04	5.11	5.19	5.26	5.34	5.42	5.49	5.57	**5.65**	5.72	5.80	5.88

NOTE: These values must be *subtracted* from the observed height value.
Courtesy, Sargent-Welch Scientific Co., 7300 N. Linder Ave., Skokie, Illinois 60076.

SLING PSYCHROMETER

This apparatus consists essentially of two identical thermometers attached to a telescoping "core." Attached to the bulb of one thermometer is a short wick which is in contact with a water reservoir.

Procedure

1. Saturate wick, then pour additional water into end cap (reservoir).
2. Extract "core."
3. While holding tubular base, whirl thermometer portion for approximately 1½ minutes. Read *wet-bulb* temperature *immediately*, then read dry-bulb temperature.
4. Return thermometer "core" to base and *align* wet- and dry-bulb temperatures on calculator scales. Value is read as percent relative humidity.

The accuracy of a sling psychrometer is related in part to the velocity of air flow past the thermometer bulbs. Sources of error are most likely to be introduced by (1) slow centrifugation of insufficient duration and (2) delayed reading wet-bulb temperature.

Motor-driven, fan-type psychrometers practically eliminate both possible sources of error commonly associated with sling types. Relative humidity is read from psychometric charts (nomograms) or tables.

STATISTICAL TERMINOLOGY AND FORMULAS

Raw Scores or Data: Actual scores.

Range: Difference between largest and smallest raw scores in a group or set of data.

Mean x̄: Arithmetic average of a group or set of data.

$$\bar{x} = \frac{\Sigma x}{n}$$

Σ = summation, x = measurement, n = number of measurements

Population: A defined group.

Sample: Subgroup drawn from a population or defined group.

Parameter: A true (as opposed to obtained) measure of a population (implies an indefinitely large number of measurements).

Variable: Statistical measurement.

Independent Variable: Statistical measurement which is manipulated by the experimenter.

Dependent Variable: Statistical measurement which is *not* manipulated by the experimenter; *dependent* upon independent variable.

Standard Deviation: Measure of variation of data around the mean. Symbolized by (s) for sample or by (σ) for population.

Ungrouped data	*Grouped (arranged) data*
$S = \sqrt{\dfrac{\Sigma(x - \bar{x})^2}{n - 1}}$	$S = \sqrt{\dfrac{\Sigma(x - \bar{x})^2 f}{n - 1}}$

x = raw data, x̄ = mean = $\dfrac{\Sigma x}{n}$ or $\dfrac{\Sigma xf}{\Sigma f}$, f = frequency

Standard Error of the Mean: Measure of precision of the mean.

$$S\bar{x} = \frac{S}{\sqrt{n}} \text{ or } \frac{\sigma}{\sqrt{n}}$$

Rank Difference, rho, ρ: A correlation method describing the relation between paired variables which are ranked serially.

$$\rho = 1 - \frac{6 \Sigma d^2}{n(n^2 - 1)}$$

format: Ranked
             Variables
Individual   X   Y   d   d²

NOTE: d = difference between ranked variables; n = number of measurements.

Correlation Coefficient, r: A correlational method which describes the degree of relationship between two variables.

$$r = \frac{\Sigma XY - \frac{\Sigma X \Sigma Y}{n}}{\sqrt{\left(\Sigma X^2 - \frac{(\Sigma X)^2}{n}\right)\left(\Sigma Y^2 - \frac{(\Sigma Y)^2}{n}\right)}} \quad \text{(raw score formula)}$$

format: Variables

                    X   Y X^2 Y^2 ΣXY

Significance of Correlation Coefficients at 5 and 1% Levels

Degrees of Freedom (N − 2)	.05	.01	Degrees of Freedom (N − 2)	.05	.01
1	.997	.999	21	.413	.526
2	.950	.990	22	.404	.515
3	.878	.959	23	.396	.505
4	.811	.917	24	.388	.496
5	.754	.874	25	.381	.487
6	.707	.834	26	.374	.478
7	.666	.798	27	.367	.470
8	.632	.765	28	.361	.463
9	.602	.735	29	.355	.456
10	.576	.708	30	.349	.449
11	.553	.684	35	.325	.418
12	.532	.661	40	.304	.393
13	.514	.641	45	.288	.372
14	.497	.623	50	.273	.354
15	.482	.606	60	.250	.325
16	.468	.590	70	.232	.302
17	.456	.575	80	.217	.283
18	.444	.561	90	.205	.267
19	.433	.549	100	.195	.254
20	.423	.537			

Adapted from Fisher, R. A., and Yates, F.: *Statistical Tables for Biological, Agricultural and Medical Research,* 4th Ed. Courtesy of Oliver and Boyd, Ltd., Edinburgh, 1963

The suggested mathematical and statistical measures are adequate for the treatment of the experimental data collected during these laboratory exercises. Obviously, more robust statistical techniques could be applied; however, basic changes in experimental design would be required and greater blocks of time allotted for laboratory periods.

Aside from the reliability of the apparatus and the adequacy of the technique, the main concern of the experimenter is that of reducing the source of experimental errors. This can be accomplished by increasing the size of the sample or by increasing the number of replications. Although simple in concept, the adoption of either choice is usually not permitted, owing to the restrictive time allotment to laboratory sessions, and often presents a dilemma to the experimenter. For example, the measurement of oxygen debt requires much team work and a substantial allotment of time. A large block of time must be expended in adapting each subject to the apparatus. Although "hidden," this time expenditure is essential to the establishment of accurate control values.

The duration of experimentation is further complicated and extended by many factors, notable among which are the problems presented by the "asportual," the obese, the under-achiever, and the poorly motivated types. Understandably, studies of this type are characterized by a small number of subjects, but by a sizeable number of replications.

By contrast, research involving reaction time or reflex latency, exemplified by short-time allotments per subject, is characterized by large sample statistics. The dilemma of choice, present in the oxygen debt example, is not operable here. This is reflected in the *Data Treatment* sections of Laboratory Exercises 11 and 12. The computation of *one* oxygen debt value is possible in Experiment 21 while the analysis of variance statistical technique is justified by the amount and type of data in Experiments 11 and 12.

Selection of an experimental method requires much thought and consideration as well as the perusal of several texts on experimental design. The guiding principle is succinctly stated by Cochran[2]: "The method adopted should be that for which the desired standard of accuracy can be attained with the smallest expenditure of time and effort. There is no special merit in either a complicated experimental plan or a highly refined technique if equally accurate results can be secured with less effort in some other way. A good working rule is to use the simplest experimental design that meets the needs of the occasion."

The interested reader would profit from a reading of Cochran,[2] especially of Chapters 1 and 2: *The Contribution of Statistics to Experimentation, Initial Steps in the Planning of Experiments, Number of Replications, Other Methods for Increasing Accuracy,* and *The Grouping of Experimental Units.* For an exalted approach to scientific investigation, Beveridge[1] is recommended.

REFERENCES

1. Beveridge, W. I. B.: *The Art of Scientific Investigation.* New York, W. W. Norton & Company, 1957.

2. Cochran, W. G.: *Experimental Designs,* 2nd Ed., New York, John Wiley & Sons, Inc., 1962.

13

Table A–2.   Relative Density and Volume of Water

Temp. °C	Density	Volume
4	1.00000	1.00000
5	0.99999	1.00001
6	997	003
7	993	007
8	988	012
9	981	019
10	0.99973	1.00027
11	963	037
12	952	048
13	940	060
14	927	073
15	0.99913	1.00087
16	897	103
17	880	120
18	862	138
19	843	157
20	0.99823	1.00177
21	802	198
22	780	221
23	756	244
24	732	268
25	0.99707	1.00294
26	681	320
27	654	347
28	626	375
29	597	405
30	0.99567	1.00435
31	537	466
32	505	497
33	473	530
34	440	563
35	0.99406	1.00598
36	371	633
37	336	669
38	299	706
39	262	743
40	0.99224	1.00782

From *Handbook of Chemistry and Physics.* Courtesy of
The Chemical Rubber Publishing Co., Cleveland Ohio.

Table A–3. Factors for Converting Body Volume into Mass

Body Segment	Segment Mass = Vol. × Mean Density	Prox.-Dist. Ratio-to-C. G.	Segment Limits
Arm	vol. × 1.07	43.6–56.4 (approx. 3–4)	Gleno-humeral to elbow center
Forearm	vol. × 1.125	43.0–57.0 (approx. 3–4)	Elbow to wrist center
Hand	vol. × 1.155	50.6–49.4 (approx. 1–1)	Wrist center to III knuckle (position of rest)
Thigh	vol. × 1.05	43.4–56.7 (approx. 3–4)	Hip to knee center
Leg	vol. × 109	43.3–56.7	Knee to ankle center
Foot	vol. × 1.095	43.9–57.1 (approx. 3–4)	Heel to toe
Trunk	Trunk mass = Total mass minus limb mass*	60.4–39.6 (approx. 3–2)	Vertex to hip joint

* Limb mass of both sides

From Dempster, W. T.: Space requirements of the seated operator: geometrical, kinematic, and mechanical aspects of the body with special reference to the limbs. WADC Technical Report 55-159, Wright Air Development Center, Air Research and Development Command, U.S.A.F., Wright-Patterson AFB, Ohio, July 1955.

Table A-4

Cooling Power of Wind Expressed as "Equivalent Chill Temperature"

Legend (diamond): °C (upper) / °F (lower)

Equivalent Chill Temperature

Each cell is given as °C / °F.

Wind Speed km/h	knots	mph	4.4 / 40	1.7 / 35	-1.1 / 30	-3.9 / 25	-6.7 / 20	-9.4 / 15	-12.2 / 10	-15.0 / 5	-17.8 / 0	-20.6 / -5	-23.3 / -10	-26.1 / -15	-28.9 / -20	-31.7 / -25
calm	calm	calm	4.4 / 40	1.7 / 35	-1.1 / 30	-3.9 / 25	-6.7 / 20	-9.4 / 15	-12.2 / 10	-15.0 / 5	-17.8 / 0	-20.6 / -5	-23.3 / -10	-26.1 / -15	-28.9 / -20	-31.7 / -25
8.05	3–6	5	1.7 / 35	-1.1 / 30	-3.9 / 25	-6.7 / 20	-9.4 / 15	-12.2 / 10	-15.0 / 5	-17.8 / 0	-20.6 / -5	-23.3 / -10	-26.1 / -15	-28.9 / -20	-31.7 / -25	-34.4 / -30
16.1	7–10	10	-1.1 / 30	-6.7 / 20	-9.4 / 15	-12.2 / 10	-15.0 / 5	-17.8 / 0	-23.3 / -10	-26.1 / -15	-28.9 / -20	-31.7 / -25	-37.2 / -35	-40.0 / -40	-42.8 / -45	-45.5 / -50
24.1	11–15	15	-3.9 / 25	-9.4 / 15	-12.2 / 10	-17.8 / 0	-20.6 / -5	-23.3 / -10	-28.9 / -20	-31.7 / -25	-34.4 / -30	-40.0 / -40	-42.8 / -45	-45.5 / -50	-51.1 / -60	-53.9 / -65
32.2	16–19	20	-6.7 / 20	-12.2 / 10	-15.0 / 5	-20.6 / -5	-23.3 / -10	-26.1 / -15	-31.8 / -25	-34.4 / -30	-37.2 / -35	-42.8 / -45	-45.5 / -50	-51.1 / -60	-53.9 / -65	-59.4 / -75
40.2	20–23	25	-9.4 / 15	-12.2 / 10	-17.8 / 0	-20.6 / -5	-26.1 / -15	-28.9 / -20	-34.4 / -30	-37.2 / -35	-42.8 / -45	-45.5 / -50	-51.1 / -60	-53.9 / -65	-59.4 / -75	-62.2 / -80
48.3	24–28	30	-12.2 / 10	-15.0 / 5	-17.8 / 0	-23.3 / -10	-28.9 / -20	-31.8 / -25	-34.4 / -30	-40.0 / -40	-45.5 / -50	-48.3 / -55	-53.9 / -65	-53.9 / -65	-62.2 / -80	-65.0 / -85
56.3	29–32	35	-12.2 / 10	-15.0 / 5	-20.6 / -5	-23.3 / -10	-28.9 / -20	-34.4 / -30	-37.2 / -35	-40.0 / -40	-45.5 / -50	-51.1 / -60	-53.9 / -65	-59.4 / -75	-62.4 / -80	-67.6 / -90
64.4	33–36	40	-12.2 / 10	-17.8 / 0	-20.6 / -5	-26.1 / -15	-28.9 / -20	-34.4 / -30	-37.2 / -35	-42.8 / -45	-48.3 / -55	-51.1 / -60	-56.6 / -70	-59.4 / -75	-65.0 / -85	-70.6 / -95

Higher wind speed has little additional effect

Little Danger	Increasing Danger (Flesh may freeze within 1 min)	Great Danger (Flesh may freeze within 30 sec)

Danger of Freezing Exposed Flesh for Properly Clothed Persons

Adapted from *Combat Crew* 18:1968. Strategic Air Command. Courtesy U.S. Air Force.

LOGARITHMS

The common logarithm, or log, of a number is expressed exponentially as the power to which a base of 10 must be raised to equal the number. (Base 10 is variously called common or Briggsian logarithm in contrast to another base 2.718, and designated by the letter e, which gives rise to a log system required in higher mathematics. This latter form is called natural, or Naperian, or hyperbolic.)

Common logarithms consist of two parts—an integer, or whole number portion, which is called the *characteristic*, and a decimal portion which is called the *mantissa*. It is well to remember that the following table of common logarithms contains only the *mantissas*—which are always positive; the *characteristic* is easily determined mentally.

To refresh the mind of the reader, some guidelines are offered:

1. The *characteristic* of *whole* numbers is *one less* than the number of figures to the *left* of the decimal point. Thus:

Number	Characteristic
784.0	2
41.0	1
81,412.0	4

2. The *characteristic* of *decimal* numbers is *minus* and is equal to the number of places (to the *right*) which are between the *decimal* point and the *first* significant number. NOTE: The *negative* characteristic is noted by a *minus sign* which appears above the characteristic. Thus:

Number	Characteristic
0.784	$\bar{1}$
0.0041	$\bar{3}$
0.00081	$\bar{4}$

3. The *mantissa*, always positive, is found in the *Table of Logarithms* by first utilizing the vertical column (labeled N) followed by the horizontal column. It is *not* related to the position of the decimal point. For example, *mantissa* portion of log 7380 = 8681. (See Table A–5.)

Example:

Find		Characteristic (see step 1)	From Table A–5	Log
Log	29.9	1	4757	1.4757
Log	784.0	2	8943	2.8943
		(see step 2)		
Log	0.0245	$\bar{2}$	3892	$\bar{2}$.3892
Log	0.000649	$\bar{4}$	8122	$\bar{4}$.8122

187

4. Interpolation. Table A–5 is not as complete as the "Five Place Log" tables found, e.g., in *The Handbook of Chemistry and Physics*, but it is adequate and gives the reader the opportunity to interpolate.

Example: Find the log of 2175. Characteristic is 3. Mantissas for 2180 and 2170 are available.

$$
\begin{aligned}
2180 &= .3385 \\
2170 &= .3365 \\
\text{difference} &= \overline{.0020}
\end{aligned}
$$

$$
\frac{5}{10} \times .0020 = .0010
$$

$$
\therefore \log 2175 = .0010 + .3365
$$

$$
\log 2175 = 3.3375
$$

5. The antilogarithm, the number which corresponds to a given logarithm, is found by locating in a log table the number corresponding to the mantissa. The position of the decimal point is determined from the characteristic. This is the reverse procedure from that followed in step 3 (see Table A–5), thus:

Number	Represented in Table A–5 by	Note
1.7938	62.2	Characteristic is 1 $\therefore$ decimal point is established 2 places from the *left* (to the right)

In many cases interpolation is necessary.

Number	From Table A–5
$\overline{2}.3294$	It is established that the first 3 figures of antilog are 213

$$
\begin{array}{ccc}
214 & 3304 & 3294 \\
213 & 3284 & 3284 \\
     & \overline{0020} & \overline{0010}
\end{array}
$$

$$
\frac{0010}{0020} = 5 \text{ attached to } 213 = 2135,
$$

antilog determined by characteristic $\overline{2}$

$$
\therefore \text{ antilog } \overline{2}.3294 = .02135 \text{ (note: reverse of step 2 above).}
$$

6. To multiply, merely add logarithms, then find the antilog which corresponds to the sum.

7. To divide, merely subtract the log of the divisor from the log of the dividend, then find the antilog of the difference. The reader may wish to use the slide rule—itself a graphic logarithmic scale—rather than the logarithmic table. The slide rule is accurate to three places.

Table A–5
Common Logarithms

N.	0	1	2	3	4	5	6	7	8	9
10	0000	0043	0086	0128	0170	0212	0253	0294	0334	0374
11	0414	0453	0492	0531	0569	0607	0645	0682	0719	0755
12	0792	0828	0864	0899	0934	0969	1004	1038	1072	1106
13	1139	1173	1206	1239	1271	1303	1335	1367	1399	1430
14	1461	1492	1523	1553	1584	1614	1644	1673	1703	1732
15	1761	1790	1818	1847	1875	1903	1931	1959	1987	2014
16	2041	2068	2095	2122	2148	2175	2201	2227	2253	2279
17	2304	2330	2355	2380	2405	2430	2455	2480	2504	2529
18	2553	2577	2601	2625	2648	2672	2695	2718	2742	2765
19	2788	2810	2833	2856	2878	2900	2923	2945	2967	2989
20	3010	3032	3054	3075	3096	3118	3139	3160	3181	3201
21	3222	3243	3263	3284	3304	3324	3345	3365	3385	3404
22	3424	3444	3464	3483	3502	3522	3541	3560	3579	3598
23	3617	3636	3655	3674	3692	3711	3729	3747	3766	3784
24	3802	3820	3838	3856	3874	3892	3909	3927	3945	3962
25	3979	3997	4014	4031	4048	4065	4082	4099	4116	4133
26	4150	4166	4183	4200	4216	4232	4249	4265	4281	4298
27	4314	4330	4346	4362	4378	4393	4409	4425	4440	4456
28	4472	4487	4502	4518	4533	4548	4564	4579	4594	4609
29	4624	4639	4654	4669	4683	4698	4713	4728	4742	4757
30	4771	4786	4800	4814	4829	4843	4857	4871	4886	4900
31	4914	4928	4942	4955	4969	4983	4997	5011	5024	5038
32	5051	5065	5079	5092	5105	5119	5132	5145	5159	5172
33	5185	5198	5211	5224	5237	5250	5263	5276	5289	5302
34	5315	5328	5340	5353	5366	5378	5391	5403	5416	5428
35	5441	5453	5465	5478	5490	5502	5514	5527	5539	5551
36	5563	5575	5587	5599	5611	5623	5635	5647	5658	5670
37	5682	5694	5705	5717	5729	5740	5752	5763	5775	5786
38	5798	5809	5821	5832	5843	5855	5866	5877	5888	5899
39	5911	5922	5933	5944	5955	5966	5977	5988	5999	6010
40	6021	6031	6042	6053	6064	6075	6085	6096	6107	6117
41	6128	6138	6149	6160	6170	6180	6191	6201	6212	6222
42	6232	6243	6253	6263	6274	6284	6294	6304	6314	6325
43	6335	6345	6355	6365	6375	6385	6395	6405	6415	6425
44	6435	6444	6454	6464	6474	6484	6493	6503	6513	6522
45	6532	6542	6551	6561	6571	6580	6590	6599	6609	6618
46	6628	6637	6646	6656	6665	6675	6684	6693	6702	6712
47	6721	6730	6739	6749	6758	6767	6776	6785	6794	6803
48	6812	6821	6830	6839	6848	6857	6866	6875	6884	6893
49	6902	6911	6920	6928	6937	6946	6955	6964	6972	6981
50	6990	6998	7007	7016	7024	7033	7042	7050	7059	7067
51	7076	7084	7093	7101	7110	7118	7126	7135	7143	7152
52	7160	7168	7177	7185	7193	7202	7210	7218	7226	7235
53	7243	7251	7259	7267	7275	7284	7292	7300	7308	7316
54	7324	7332	7340	7348	7356	7364	7372	7380	7388	7396
N.	0	1	2	3	4	5	6	7	8	9

COMMON LOGARITHMS.—*(Continued)*

N.	0	1	2	3	4	5	6	7	8	9
55	7404	7412	7419	7427	7435	7443	7451	7459	7466	7474
56	7482	7490	7497	7505	7513	7520	7528	7536	7543	7551
57	7559	7566	7574	7582	7589	7597	7604	7612	7619	7627
58	7634	7642	7649	7657	7664	7672	7679	7686	7694	7701
59	7709	7716	7723	7731	7738	7745	7752	7760	7767	7774
60	7782	7789	7796	7803	7810	7818	7825	7832	7839	7846
61	7853	7860	7868	7875	7882	7889	7896	7903	7910	7917
62	7924	7931	7938	7945	7952	7959	7966	7973	7980	7987
63	7993	8000	8007	8014	8021	8028	8035	8041	8048	8055
64	8062	8069	8075	8082	8089	8096	8102	8109	8116	8122
65	8129	8136	8142	8149	8156	8162	8169	8176	8182	8189
66	8195	8202	8209	8215	8222	8228	8235	8241	8248	8254
67	8261	8267	8274	8280	8287	8293	8299	8306	8312	8319
68	8325	8331	8338	8344	8351	8357	8363	8370	8376	8382
69	8388	8395	8401	8407	8414	8420	8426	8432	8439	8445
70	8451	8457	8463	8470	8476	8482	8488	8494	8500	8506
71	8513	8519	8525	8531	8537	8543	8549	8555	8561	8567
72	8573	8579	8585	8591	8597	8603	8609	8615	8621	8627
73	8633	8639	8645	8651	8657	8663	8669	8675	8681	8686
74	8692	8698	8704	8710	8716	8722	8727	8733	8739	8745
75	8751	8756	8762	8768	8774	8779	8785	8791	8797	8802
76	8808	8814	8820	8825	8831	8837	8842	8848	8854	8859
77	8865	8871	8876	8882	8887	8893	8899	8904	8910	8915
78	8921	8927	8932	8938	8943	8949	8954	8960	8965	8971
79	8976	8982	8987	8993	8998	9004	9009	9015	9020	9025
80	9031	9036	9042	9047	9053	9058	9063	9069	9074	9079
81	9085	9090	9096	9101	9106	9112	9117	9122	9128	9133
82	9138	9143	9149	9154	9159	9165	9170	9175	9180	9186
83	9191	9196	9201	9206	9212	9217	9222	9227	9232	9238
84	9243	9248	9253	9258	9263	9269	9274	9279	9284	9289
85	9294	9299	9304	9309	9315	9320	9325	9330	9335	9340
86	9345	9350	9355	9360	9365	9370	9375	9380	9385	9390
87	9395	9400	9405	9410	9415	9420	9425	9430	9435	9440
88	9445	9450	9455	9460	9465	9469	9474	9479	9484	9489
89	9494	9499	9504	9509	9513	9518	9523	9528	9533	9538
90	9542	9547	9552	9557	9562	9566	9571	9576	9581	9586
91	9590	9595	9600	9605	9609	9614	9619	9624	9628	9633
92	9638	9643	9647	9652	9657	9661	9666	9671	9675	9680
93	9685	9689	9694	9699	9703	9708	9713	9717	9722	9727
94	9731	9736	9741	9745	9750	9754	9759	9763	9768	9773
95	9777	9782	9786	9791	9795	9800	9805	9809	9814	9818
96	9823	9827	9832	9836	9841	9845	9850	9854	9859	9863
97	9868	9872	9877	9881	9886	9890	9894	9899	9903	9908
98	9912	9917	9921	9926	9930	9934	9939	9943	9948	9952
99	9956	9961	9965	9969	9974	9978	9983	9987	9991	9996
N.	0	1	2	3	4	5	6	7	8	9

NATURAL TRIGONOMETRIC FUNCTIONS

Degrees	SINES							Cosines
	0′	10′	20′	30′	40′	50′	60′	
0	0.00000	0.00291	0.00582	0.00873	0.01164	0.01454	0.01745	89
1	0.01745	0.02036	0.02327	0.02618	0.02908	0.03199	0.03490	88
2	0.03490	0.03781	0.04071	0.04362	0.04653	0.04943	0.05234	87
3	0.05234	0.05524	0.05814	0.06105	0.06395	0.06685	0.06976	86
4	0.06976	0.07266	0.07556	0.07846	0.08136	0.08426	0.08716	85
5	0.08716	0.09005	0.09295	0.09585	0.09874	0.10164	0.10453	84
6	0.10453	0.10742	0.11031	0.11320	0.11609	0.11898	0.12187	83
7	0.12187	0.12476	0.12764	0.13053	0.13341	0.13629	0.13917	82
8	0.13917	0.14205	0.14493	0.14781	0.15069	0.15356	0.15643	81
9	0.15643	0.15931	0.16218	0.16505	0.16792	0.17078	0.17365	80
10	0.17365	0.17651	0.17937	0.18224	0.18509	0.18795	0.19081	79
11	0.19081	0.19366	0.19652	0.19937	0.20222	0.20507	0.20791	78
12	0.20791	0.21076	0.21360	0.21644	0.21928	0.22212	0.22495	77
13	0.22495	0.22778	0.23062	0.23345	0.23627	0.23910	0.24192	76
14	0.24192	0.24474	0.24756	0.25038	0.25320	0.25601	0.25882	75
15	0.25882	0.26163	0.26443	0.26724	0.27004	0.27284	0.27564	74
16	0.27564	0.27843	0.28123	0.28402	0.28680	0.28959	0.29237	73
17	0.29237	0.29515	0.29793	0.30071	0.30348	0.30625	0.30902	72
18	0.30902	0.31178	0.31454	0.31730	0.32006	0.32282	0.32557	71
19	0.32557	0.32832	0.33106	0.33381	0.33655	0.33929	0.34202	70
20	0.34202	0.34475	0.34748	0.35021	0.35293	0.35565	0.35837	69
21	0.35837	0.36108	0.36379	0.36650	0.36921	0.37191	0.37461	68
22	0.37461	0.37730	0.37999	0.38268	0.38537	0.38805	0.39073	67
23	0.39073	0.39341	0.39608	0.39875	0.40142	0.40408	0.40674	66
24	0.40674	0.40939	0.41204	0.41469	0.41734	0.41998	0.42262	65
25	0.42262	0.42525	0.42788	0.43051	0.43313	0.43575	0.43837	64
26	0.43837	0.44098	0.44359	0.44620	0.44880	0.45140	0.45399	63
27	0.45399	0.45658	0.45917	0.46175	0.46433	0.46690	0.46947	62
28	0.46947	0.47204	0.47460	0.47716	0.47971	0.48226	0.48481	61
29	0.48481	0.48735	0.48989	0.49242	0.49495	0.49748	0.50000	60
30	0.50000	0.50252	0.50503	0.50754	0.51004	0.51254	0.51504	59
31	0.51504	0.51753	0.52002	0.52250	0.52498	0.52745	0.52992	58
32	0.52992	0.53238	0.53484	0.53730	0.53975	0.54220	0.54464	57
33	0.54464	0.54708	0.54951	0.55194	0.55436	0.55678	0.55919	56
34	0.55919	0.56160	0.56401	0.56641	0.56880	0.57119	0.57358	55
35	0.57358	0.57596	0.57833	0.58070	0.58307	0.58543	0.58779	54
36	0.58779	0.59014	0.59248	0.59482	0.59716	0.59949	0.60182	53
37	0.60182	0.60414	0.60645	0.60876	0.61107	0.61337	0.61566	52
38	0.61566	0.61795	0.62024	0.62251	0.62479	0.62706	0.62932	51
39	0.62932	0.63158	0.63383	0.63608	0.63832	0.64056	0.64279	50
40	0.64279	0.64501	0.64723	0.64945	0.65166	0.65386	0.65606	49
41	0.65606	0.65825	0.66044	0.66262	0.66480	0.66697	0.66913	48
42	0.66913	0.67129	0.67344	0.67559	0.67773	0.67987	0.68200	47
43	0.68200	0.68412	0.68624	0.68835	0.69046	0.69256	0.69466	46
44	0.69466	0.69675	0.69883	0.70091	0.70298	0.70505	0.70711	45
Sines	60′	50′	40′	30′	20′	10′	0′	Degrees
	COSINES							

Natural Trigonometric Functions

Degrees	COSINES							Sines
	0′	10′	20′	30′	40′	50′	60′	
0	1.00000	1.00000	0.99998	0.99996	0.99993	0.99989	0.99985	89
1	0.99985	0.99979	0.99973	0.99966	0.99958	0.99949	0.99939	88
2	0.99939	0.99929	0.99917	0.99905	0.99892	0.99878	0.99863	87
3	0.99863	0.99847	0.99831	0.99813	0.99795	0.99776	0.99756	86
4	0.99756	0.99736	0.99714	0.99692	0.99668	0.99644	0.99619	85
5	0.99619	0.99594	0.99567	0.99540	0.99511	0.99482	0.99452	84
6	0.99452	0.99421	0.99390	0.99357	0.99324	0.99290	0.99255	83
7	0.99255	0.99219	0.99182	0.99144	0.99106	0.99067	0.99027	82
8	0.99027	0.98986	0.98944	0.98902	0.98858	0.98814	0.98769	81
9	0.98769	0.98723	0.98676	0.98629	0.98580	0.98531	0.98481	80
10	0.98481	0.98430	0.98378	0.98325	0.98272	0.98218	0.98163	79
11	0.98163	0.98107	0.98050	0.97992	0.97934	0.97875	0.97815	78
12	0.97815	0.97754	0.97692	0.97630	0.97566	0.97502	0.97437	77
13	0.97437	0.97371	0.97304	0.97237	0.97169	0.97100	0.97030	76
14	0.97030	0.96959	0.96887	0.96815	0.96742	0.96667	0.96593	75
15	0.96593	0.96517	0.96440	0.96363	0.96285	0.96206	0.96126	74
16	0.96126	0.96046	0.95964	0.95882	0.95799	0.95715	0.95630	73
17	0.95630	0.95545	0.95459	0.95372	0.95284	0.95195	0.95106	72
18	0.95106	0.95015	0.94924	0.94832	0.94740	0.94646	0.94552	71
19	0.94552	0.94457	0.94361	0.94264	0.94167	0.94068	0.93969	70
20	0.93969	0.93869	0.93769	0.93667	0.93565	0.93462	0.93358	69
21	0.93358	0.93253	0.93148	0.93042	0.92935	0.92827	0.92718	68
22	0.92718	0.92609	0.92499	0.92388	0.92276	0.92164	0.92050	67
23	0.92050	0.91936	0.91822	0.91706	0.91590	0.91472	0.91355	66
24	0.91355	0.91236	0.91116	0.90996	0.90875	0.90753	0.90631	65
25	0.90631	0.90507	0.90383	0.90259	0.90133	0.90007	0.89879	64
26	0.89879	0.89752	0.89623	0.89493	0.89363	0.89232	0.89101	63
27	0.89101	0.88968	0.88835	0.88701	0.88566	0.88431	0.88295	62
28	0.88295	0.88158	0.88020	0.87882	0.87743	0.87603	0.87462	61
29	0.87462	0.87321	0.87178	0.87036	0.86892	0.86748	0.86603	60
30	0.86603	0.86457	0.86310	0.86163	0.86015	0.85866	0.85717	59
31	0.85717	0.85567	0.85416	0.85264	0.85112	0.84959	0.84805	58
32	0.84805	0.84650	0.84495	0.84339	0.84182	0.84025	0.83867	57
33	0.83867	0.83708	0.83549	0.83389	0.83228	0.83066	0.82904	56
34	0.82904	0.82741	0.82577	0.82413	0.82248	0.82082	0.81915	55
35	0.81915	0.81748	0.81580	0.81412	0.81242	0.81072	0.80902	54
36	0.80902	0.80730	0.80558	0.80386	0.80212	0.80038	0.79864	53
37	0.79864	0.79688	0.79512	0.79335	0.79158	0.78980	0.78801	52
38	0.78801	0.78622	0.78442	0.78261	0.78079	0.77897	0.77715	51
39	0.77715	0.77531	0.77347	0.77162	0.76977	0.76791	0.76604	50
40	0.76604	0.76417	0.76229	0.76041	0.75851	0.75661	0.75471	49
41	0.75471	0.75280	0.75088	0.74896	0.74703	0.74509	0.74314	48
42	0.74314	0.74120	0.73924	0.73728	0.73531	0.73333	0.73135	47
43	0.73135	0.72937	0.72737	0.72537	0.72337	0.72136	0.71934	46
44	0.71934	0.71732	0.71529	0.71325	0.71121	0.70916	0.70711	45
Cosines	60′	50′	40′	30′	20′	10′	0′	Degrees

SINES

APPENDIX B

**Laboratory Exercise Number 1—Estimation
of Body Fat, Behnke Technique**

Required Apparatus	*Approximate Cost*
Anthropometer or shoulder breadth caliper (metric units)*	$45.00
Scale, physician's type with stadiometer	75.00

**Laboratory Exercise Number 2—Estimation of
Body Surface Area: DuBois Height-Weight Formula**

Required Apparatus	*Approximate Cost*
Scale, physician's type with stadiometer	$75.00

**Laboratory Exercise Number 3—Estimation of Specific Gravity:
Archimedian Principle, Behnke, Feen, and Welham Technique**

Required Apparatus and Materials	*Approximate Cost*
Scale (autopsy type, without pan)	$120.00 (15 kg × 25 gm†)
Scale suspension frame (see Fig. 2–3)	25.00 (local construction) (includes circular metal seat and chain)
Weight belt (scuba accessory) (5 kg)	18.00

* Suggested source: J. A. Preston Corp., 71 Fifth Avenue, New York, N. Y. 10003.
† This type features air dashpots which serve to absorb shock loads and bring pointer to quick rest; 13-inch dial. A lower priced 9-inch dial is available but this does not include dashpots. Source: John Chatillon and Sons, Division of Aero-Chatillon Corp., 83–30 Kew Gardens Road, Kew Gardens, N. Y. 11415.

Scale, physician's type, with stadiometer	75.00
Spirometer, recording type, Collins (see p. 127)	625.00, 9 liter; 835.00 13.5 liter
Nose clip	2.50
Swimming pool equipped with 1-meter diving board (for scale suspension frame)	

OR

Backyard type, above ground, circular pool,* 12-gauge vinyl, of sufficient volume to contain completely submerged body	75.00 to 285.00

Laboratory Exercise Number 4—Estimation of Systolic and Diastolic Blood Pressure and the Recording and Demonstration of Variability of Cardiac Frequency and Pulse Rate

Required Apparatus	*Approximate Cost*
Stethoscope	$ 3.50
Sphygmomanometer, mercurial type (quick release coupling is advocated between inflatable bag and inflating bulb)	50.00
Plinth	40.00
Electric wall clock with sweep-second hand (12-inch diameter dial)	15.00

Laboratory Exercise Number 5—The Hyman Index: An Index of the Adjustment Capability of the Heart

The *required apparatus* is the same as that for Laboratory Exercise Number 4.

Laboratory Exercise Number 6—Carlson Fatigue Curve Test

Required Apparatus	*Approximate Cost*
Electric wall clock with sweep-second hand	$15.00

* 10 feet × 30 feet complete with filter, $75.00; 18 feet × 48 feet, complete with filter, $285.00. Source: Sears, Roebuck and Co.

Laboratory Exercise Number 7—Cardiac Adjustment to Change in Rate and Amount of Work

Required Apparatus	*Approximate Cost*
2 Benches; one 20.3 cm in height; one 40.6 cm in height. Both benches 2 meters in length and 30.5 cm in width	$ 8.00 Lumber cost; benches assembled locally
1 Electric metronome (40–208 strokes/min)	20.00
1 Stethoscope	3.50
1 Electric wall clock with sweep-second hand	15.00
1 Scale, physician's type with stadiometer	75.00

Laboratory Exercise Number 8—Interrelationship of Load and Cadence to Girth of Forearm Flexors

Required Apparatus and Materials	*Approximate Cost*
Electric metronome (40–208 strokes/min)	$20.00
Dumb bells (2 kg, 5 kg)	8.00
Electric wall clock with sweep-second hand	15.00
Gulick tape*	12.00
Plethysmograph	Local construction
Skin marking pencil	0.10

Laboratory Exercise Number 9—Force Analysis in Knee Extension

Required Apparatus and Materials	*Approximate Cost*
Gulick tape*	$12.00
Plethysmograph	Local construction
Goniometer (plastic)	4.00
Skin-marking pencil	0.10

* Suggested source; J. A. Preston Corp., 71 Fifth Avenue, New York, N. Y. 10003.

Laboratory Exercise Number 10—
Measuring Reaction Time RT and Movement Time MT

Required Apparatus and Materials	*Approximate Cost*
2 Precision Timers* @ $90.00 each	$180.00
1 Lever switch, multiple circuit	5.00
1 Microswitch push button or leaf	2.50
1 Double-pole single-throw switch	0.50
Copper conducting hook-up wire (at least 4 different colors of outer insulation preferred)	3.00
4 No. 15 dry cells (1.5 volt each) @ 75¢ each	3.00
1 Buzzer or bell, 6 volt	1.75
4 Minigators, insulated alligator clips @12½¢ each	0.50
3 Jiffy box chassis 4 inches in length, 2 inches wide, 2¾ inches in depth, @ $.75	2.25

Laboratory Exercise Number 11—Effect of Heat and of Cold
on Reaction Time and Movement Time of Preferred Limb

The *required apparatus* is the same as that for Laboratory Exercise Number 10.

Laboratory Exercise Number 12—Effect of Normal versus Reduced
Blood Flow in Upper Limb on Reaction Time and Movement Time

Required Apparatus and Materials	*Approximate Cost*
Same requirement as for Laboratory Exercise Number 10 plus the following:	
Sphygmomanometer, mercurial type	$50.00

*Standard Electric Time Co., Springfield, Mass. 01101. Model S1 115V-60 cycles a.c., manual reset. (Electric reset models are also available at additional cost.)

Laboratory Exercise Number 13—Estimation of Range of Movement of Left Knee and Ankle during Bench Stepping

Required Apparatus and Materials	*Approximate Cost*
Two-channel control circuit* includes elgons, protractor, and chassis (base to which components are attached)	$ 35.00
2 Elgon chasses including brass hinges (½ inch × ⅞₁₆ inch wide open), snap fasteners	1.00
Recorder, two channel minimum	1000.00
Adhesive tape, 1-inch width	0.25 roll
Skin marking pencil	0.10
Wooden bench	Local construction

Laboratory Exercise Number 14—Heat Production and Avenues of Heat Loss during Exercise

Required Apparatus and Materials	*Approximate Cost*
Tele-thermometer,† 6 channel, 0° to 51° C, including 6 probes:	$400.00
1 physiological	14.00
5 surface temperature (@ 21.00 each)	105.00
Clinical (oral) thermometer	1.50
Thermometer (−1 to 20° C)	2.50
Surgical tape,‡ roll: 12.7 mm × 4.57 m	.60
Sling psychrometer (see p. 180)	14.00
Physician's scale	75.00
Electric metronome (40–208 strokes/min)	20.00
2 Sweat shirts (see Fig. 7–2)	7.00

*NOTE: A single channel is depicted in Figure 6–1. Additional channels would NOT require additional microammeters or batteries but would require the remaining parts depicted. These would be wired in parallel circuitry with the battery source and microammeter. The price of the microammeter is approximately $17.00.

† Yellow Springs Instruments Co., Yellow Springs, Ohio 45387.

‡ Blenderm, a product of 3M Company.

1 Sweat trousers   4.50

Bench—20.3 cm   Local construction

Miscellaneous items
  200 cc alcohol, 70%
  2 Towels
  Orange juice, frozen concentrate

  Thermos bottle, 2 qt.
  2 Small paper cups
  Gauze pads

Laboratory Exercise Number 15—Sweat Loss and Composition

Required Apparatus and Materials	*Approximate Cost*
Tele-thermometer, 6-channel, 0–51° C, including 1 physiological probe and 5 surface temperature probes	$519.00
Sling psychrometer (see Appendix p. 180)	14.00
Physician's scale	75.00
Electric metronome (40–208 strokes/min)	20.00
Cloth sweat shirt and trousers	8.00
Plastic (vinyl) sweat shirt and trousers	5.00
Surgical tape, roll (12.7 mm × 4.57 m)	.60
Hydrogen ion test paper, short-range comparators to span pH range 4.0 to 7.0	2.00 roll
Bench 40.6 cm	Local construction

Miscellaneous items:
  200 cc alcohol, 70%
  Gauze pads
  2 Towels

Laboratory Exercise Number 16—Effect of Exercise on Urine Volume and Composition

Required Apparatus	*Approximate Cost*
Urine specimen bottles, graduated	$ 0.25 each

3 Urinometers, approx. 12-ml size @ $4.00	12.00
Hydrogen ion test papers, short-range comparators to span pH range 4.0 to 8.0	2.00
Reagent strips, Labstix* bottle (125)	9.00
Karo syrup† 1 pint	0.35
Distilled water, 1000 ml	

Laboratory Exercise Number 17—Subdivisions of Lung Volume Taken in the Erect Standing Position

Required Apparatus and Materials	*Approximate Cost*
Recording spirometer‡ with 3-speed kymograph	$625.00 (9 Liter) 835.00 (13.5 Liter)
Barometer, mercurial	60.00
Nose clips	2.50
Mouthpiece, rubber‡	1.50
Oxygen, USP (300 cu ft cylinder)	6.50
Regulator	40.00
Alcohol, 70% solution	

Laboratory Exercise Number 18—Vital Capacity: One-Stage, Two-Stage, Timed, Predicted. Comparisons of Minute Volume Measurement

Required Apparatus and Materials	*Approximate Cost*
Same requirement as for Laboratory Exercise Number 17 plus the following:	
Stadiometer (on physician's scale)	$75.00
Shoulder breadth caliper	45.00

*Produced by Ames Company, Inc. Elkhart Indiana 46514. Also available are Combustix, reagent strips for protein, glucose, and pH, or as Clinistix® for specific qualitative tests.

† Karo syrup (Corn Products Company) is available at most food stores.

‡ Suggested source: Warren E. Collins, Inc., 220 Wood Road, Braintree, Massachusetts 02184.

Laboratory Exercise Number 19—Effect of Various Gas Mixtures on External Respiration

Required Apparatus and Materials	*Approximate Cost*
Same requirement as for Laboratory Exercise Number 18 plus the following:	
Carbon dioxide cylinder (60-lb.) purity 99.5%	$ 8.00
Regulator	40.00

Laboratory Exercise Number 20—Calculating Oxygen Consumption $\dot{V}o_2$, Ventilation Equivalent for Oxygen VEo$_2$, and Reciprocal of VEo$_2$ by Means of Closed-Circuit Systems

Required Apparatus and Materials	*Approximate Cost*
Recording spirometer* with 3-speed kymograph	$625.00 (9-liter) 835.00 (13.5-liter)
Barometer, mercury†	60.00
Nose clip	2.50
Mouthpiece, rubber*	1.50
Oxygen cylinder (300 cu ft) purity: USP	6.50
Regulator	40.00
Alcohol, 70% solution	

Laboratory Exercise Number 21—Calculating Oxygen Consumption by the Open-Circuit Method

Required Apparatus and Materials	*Approximate Cost*
Scholander gas analyzer‡	$200.00
Glassware, miscellaneous	75.00

*Suggested source: Warren E. Collins, Inc., 220 Wood Road, Braintree, Massachusetts 02184.

† Suggested source: Sargent-Welch Scientific Co., 7300 N. Linder Ave., Skokie, Illinois 60076.

‡ Suggested source: Otto K. Hebel, Scientific Instruments, 80 Swarthmore Ave., Rutledge, Pennsylvania 19070.

Apparatus* for open-circuit assessment,
  bag collection method:

Dry gas meter with centigrade thermometer	155.00
Nose clip	2.50
Two-way J valve	45.00
4 Stopcocks, T-shape (3-way tap), aluminum @ $25.00 each	100.00
3 Gas bags, Douglas type, 150 L, @ 110.00 each	330.00
British cloth-covered, corrugated tubing, 24-inch (1 inch ID)	9.00
Smooth rubber tubing, 12-inch (¾ inch ID)	.75
Head band for welder's mask	4.00
Rack, for Douglas bags	Local construction
Scale, physician's	75.00
Electric wall clock with sweep-second hand	15.00
Bench, 20.3 cm	Local construction
Electric metronome (40–208 strokes/min)	20.00

Laboratory Exercise Number 22—Step-Test: A Physiological Appraisal

Required Apparatus and Materials	*Approximate Cost*
Same requirement as for Laboratory Exercise Number 21 plus the following:	
Stethoscope	$ 3.50
1 Additional Douglas bag, 150 L, fitted with sampling tubing and stopcock	135.00
Bench, 40.6 cm	Locally constructed

* Suggested source: Warren E. Collins, Inc., 220 Wood Road, Braintree, Massachusetts 02184.

INDEX

Numbers in *italics* refer to pages on which definition of the word or term is given.

ABDUCTION, *92*
Accident prevention, 13–15
Acclimation, *106*
Acclimatization, *106*
Acids, precautions in handling of, 14
Adduction, *92*
Ambient, 103, *108*
Anatomical position, 91
Apparatus and materials, suggested
   sources of, 163, 195–203
Atmosphere, composition of, 144

BAROMETER, 125, 126
   mercurial, temperature corrections for,
     178, 179
   reading of, 177–179
Behnke, constants of, 22
   derivation of, 21
   lean body weight formula of, 22, 23
Bell factor, 125, *127*
Bellows effect, *108*
Bicycle ergometer, 48, 49
Blind, double, *141*
   single, *139*
Blood pressure, 39
   diastolic, 39
   measurement of, 36–38, 40
   systolic, 39
Body density, 19, 30, 33, 185
Body fat, percent, formula for, 19, 23, 31
Body heat, balance of, 104–106
   gain of, 104
   loss of, 104, 105, 108
Body mass, factors for conversion of body
   volume into, 185
Body surface area, *25*
   DuBois' formula for, 25, 26
Body temperature, mean, Burton's form-
   ula for, 111
Body volume, factors for conversion of,
   into mass, 185

Body weight, lean, 20, 21
   Behnke's formula for determination
     of, 22, 23
BTPS, 125, 142, 145
Burton, mean body temperature formula,
   111
   weighted skin temperature formula of,
     111

CALCULATION, example, of body surface
   area, 25
   of gas percentage, Scholander, 171
   of muscle cross-section, 63, 64
   of specific gravity, 29, 30
   of torque, 66, 67
Calibration, 10–13
   graphical portrayal of discrepancy in,
     12
   tabular portrayal of discrepancy in, 12
Caloric cost, *158, 159*
Calorimetry, direct, 144–146
   indirect, open and closed, 144, 145, 151,
     155
Carbon dioxide, effect of, upon ventila-
   tion, 124
Cardiac frequency, 40, 48
Cardiac index, *159*
Cardiac output, 36, 38, 159
Carlson fatigue curve test, 45, 46
Catalog cards, library, 2
Chill temperature, equivalent, 186
Circumduction, *92*
Constants of Behnke, 22
   derivation of, 21
Control value, *139*
Coordination loss, 54
Core temperature, *107*
   reflection of, by tympanic membrane,
     120
Cost, net, *158*

DENSITY, body, 19, 30, 33, 185
  relative, and volume of water, 184
Double blind approach, *141*
Douglas bag, emptying of, 154, 174, 175, 176
  readying of, 173, 174
  withdrawal of gas sample from, 173, 175
DuBois, body surface area formula of, 25, *26*

ECTOTHERM, *104*
Efficiency, gross, *158*
  net, *158*
Effort, duration of, 57
Electrical circuits, precautions in working with, 14
Elgon, 63, 67, 89, 92, 101
  operation of, 94–97
Endotherm, *104*
Energy cost, *158*, *159*
Equivalent chill temperature, 186
Ergometer, bicycle, 48, 49
Error, percent, formula for, 41
Eversion, *92*
Exhalometer, 142
Experimental method, 182, 183
Expiratory volume, forced, see *Vital capacity, timed.*
Extension, *92*

FAT, body, percent of, formula for, 19, 23, 31
Fatigue, 57
  Carlson's curve test of, 45, 46
  sequence of measurement effects of, 59, 61
Fatigue-effect, 139
Fire extinguisher, 14
Flexion, *92*
Foot, weight of, formula for, 66
Force, muscle, 54, 56, *65*, 67, 69
  comparability of sexes, 69, 70
Forearm, weight of, formula for, 62
Formula, Behnke, lean body weight (LBW) of, 22, 23
  Burton, mean body temperature, 111
    weighted skin temperature, 111
  DuBois, body surface area, 25, *26*
  oxygen consumption, 153
  percent body fat, 19, 23, 31
  percent error, 41
  power, 62
  specific gravity of human body (Behnke, Feen, and Welham; Cowgill), 30
  weight of forearm, 62

Formula (*Continued*)
  weight of hand, 62
  weight of leg and foot, 66

GAS sample, withdrawal of, from Douglas bag, 173, 175
Goniogram, 67, *92*
Graph, condenser in, 8, 9
  construction of, 8–10
  coordinate axes of, 8
  rule of convention, 8
Gravity, specific, see *Specific gravity.*
Gross cost, *158*

HAND, weight of, formula for, 62
Harvard step-test, 36, 50, 51
Heart, see under *Cardiac.*
Heat, body, balance of, 104–106
  gain of, 104
  loss of, 104, 105, 108
Heat chamber, 114, 115
Heat exchange, law of, 103
Height-weight, charts of, 18
Hematuria, 117
Homeotherm, *104*
Humidity, relative, *108*
  determination of, 180
Hydrogen ion test papers, *112*
Hyman index, 43, 44

INNING, *45*
Inversion, *92*

JOURNALS, list of, 4–7

KETONURIA, *116*, 117
Kilopond, KPM, 48

LABORATORY apparatus, sources of, 163, 195–203
Lean body weight (LBW), *20*, *21*
Leg, weight of, formula for, 66
Library of congress classifications Q, R, Z, 2, 3
Limb, preferred, *79*
Literature search, 2
  catalog cards, 2
  Library of Congress classifications Q, R, Z, 2, 3
  oft-used references, 15
  periodicals, 3, 4
Logarithms, manipulation, 187–189
  tables, 190, 191
Lungs, elasticity of, 124

MICROCLIMATE, *108*
Minute volume, 38, *147*, 159

Moment of force, 55, 57, 62, 65, 67, 101;
see also *Torque*.
Motion, 89, 90, 102
Mouthpiece, sterilization of, 123, 143
Movement, 90
range of (ROM), 57, 91
Movement time, 76

NET cost, *158*
Net recovery oxygen, *149;* see also
Oxygen debt.

OHM's law, *92*, 107
Oxygen, effect of, upon ventilation, 124,
125
reciprocal of ventilation equivalent for,
146
Oxygen consumption, *146*
formula for, 153
Oxygen debt, *149;* see also *Net recovery*
oxygen.
Oxygen pulse, *159*

PERCENT error, 41
Periodicals, 3, 4
Perspiration, pH of, estimation of, 112
114
pH, 115, *116*
of perspiration, estimation of, 112, 114
of urine, estimation of, 112, 116, 118
Physical fitness, 50
pull-up dilemma, 55
Physiological fitness, 50
Planes, frontal or coronal, *91*
horizontal or transverse, *91, 92*
median, *91*
Plethysmograph, 57, 58
Poikilotherm, *104*
Position, anatomical, *91*
Power formula, 62
Preferred limb, 79
Production, *45*
Pronation, *92*
Proteinuria, *116*
Psychrometer, sling, *180*
Pull-ups, 55
Pulse, venous, 41
Pulse pressure, *43*
Pulse rate, 35, 40–42, 45

RANGE of movement (ROM), 57, *91*
Reaction time, 75, 85–87
Reciprocal of ventilation equivalent for
oxygen, *146*
Rectal temperature, *107*
References, oft-used, 15
Relative density and volume of water, 184

Relative humidity, *108*
determination of, 180
Reports, written, 7, 8
secondary source documentation, 8
Required apparatus and materials, ap-
proximate cost and suggested sources,
195–203
Respiration, 123–125
Respiratory exchange ratio, *159*
Respirometer, see *Spirometer, recording*.
Response time, total, 74
Rotated, 139
Rotation, *92*

SAFETY considerations, 13–15
Scholander apparatus, assembly of, 166–
168
operation of, 168–171
reagents, glassware, 165, 166
Shell temperature, *107*, 120
Single blind, *139*
Skin temperature, weighted, Burton's
formula for, 111
Skinfold thickness measurements, 33, 34
Sources of laboratory apparatus, 163,
195–203
Specific gravity, 27
calculation of, example, 29, 30
estimation of, 27
of human body, Behnke, Feen, and
Welham's formula for, 30
Cowgill's formula for, 30
of urine, 116, 117
Sphygmomanometer, 36, 82
anaeroid, 36
electronic, 37
Spirometer, recording, *127*
operation of, 127–131
Spotter, *14*
Statistical terminology and formulas, 181,
182
Stem height, 134, *135*
Step-test, Harvard, 36, 50, 51
Sterilization of mouthpieces, 123, 143
STPD, 125, 145, 153
Strain, *56*
Strain gauge (transducer), *69*
Strength, 53, 54
incompleteness of term, 54–56, 69
Stress, *56*
Supination, *92*
Surface temperature, *107*, 120

TELE-THERMOMETER, *107*
Temperature, body, mean, Burton's formula for, 111
core, *107*

Temperature, core (*Continued*)
  reflection of, by tympanic membrane,
    120
  equivalent chill, 186
  rectal, *107*
  shell, *107*, 120
  skin, weighted, Burton's formula for,
    111
  surface, *107*, 120
Temperature corrections for mercurial
  barometer, 178, 179
Thermography, 120
Torque, *57*, 65, 101; see also *Moment of
  force.*
  calculation of, examples, 66, 67
  in knee extension, 67
  in pull-ups, 55
  relation of, to flexion, 62
Torr units, 126
Total response time, 74
Transducer (strain gauge), *69*
Trigonometric functions, 192, 193
Tympanic membrane, reflection of core
  temperature by, 120

URINE, basal sample of, *117*
  pH of, estimation of, 112, 116, 118
  specific gravity of, 116, 117

Urinometer, *116*

VENOUS pulse, 41
Ventilation, 123–125
  effect of CO_2 on, 124
  effect of O_2 on, 124, 125
Ventilation equivalent for oxygen, *126*
Ventilogram, 129, *134, 135*
Vital capacity, 131
  one-stage, 31, *132*
  predicted, 132
  timed, 132, 133
  two-stage, *127, 132*
"Voice command"-triggered circuit, 84,
  85
Volatile solutions, storage of, 14

WATER, relative density and volume of,
  184
Weight, 17, 18
  lean body (LBW), 20, 21
  of foot, formula for, 66
  of forearm, formula for, 62
  of hand, formula for, 62
  of leg, formula for, 66
Weight-height, charts of, 18
Work, *47, 57*, 62, 63
  in pull-ups, 55
  in step testing, 158